The Complete Guide to Cavachons

David **Anderson**

Cover photo courtesy of Adam Ball

TABLE OF CONTENTS

INTRODUCTION

Cavachons are designer dogs that were bred to be nearly perfect companions. Both of their parent breeds, the Cavalier King Charles Spaniel and the Bichon Frise, are well-loved because of how personable and cute they are. Given how friendly and snuggly their parents are, it is no surprise that the Cavachon is an ardent cuddle pup that loves little more than to be with the family. With their small stature, they make an incredibly versatile dog that fits into any environment with ease. If you have a small home and want a dog that can easily be accommodated within a limited space, the Cavachon is perfect.

One of the initial draws to these dogs is their absolutely adorable appearance. Their large, round eyes framed between two soft ears makes them look as much like a stuffed animal as an actual dog. Their behavior is also like a stuffed dog come to life, and they want to be with you more than anything else. This makes training these adorable little dogs incredibly easy without requiring a lot of food to do it. If you enjoy training dogs, this will be one more area that you can use to show off your cute, little, fluffy bundle.

When you are sitting down and enjoying your favorite TV show, your Cavachon will happily cuddle up on your lap. Petting your pup will become a secondary reaction to sitting, and it can be very relaxing. This is one reason why Cavachons also make great therapy dogs. They tend to love everyone, and their happy energy is more sedate than other small dogs. This does not mean they don't love adventure –they just appreciate relaxing with you because being with you is what makes them happiest.

If you are the more adventurous type, the Cavachon is still a great dog to have because they are so curious. With their intelligence, they will be more than happy to go out hiking with you.

They are a designer dog, which means you need to be careful when finding the Cavachon to bring home. While the largest aspects of their personality are pretty easy to predict, the details are not. Beyond loving people and wanting to be with people all the time, their personalities depend on which parent they take after. Sometimes the personalities are more closely aligned with the energetic Cavalier King Charles Spaniel; other times they are more like the laidback Bichon Frise. Fortunately, with training, you can pretty much help mold your Cavachon into the kind of dog that will be the best companion for your lifestyle.

CHAPTER 1
A Unique Look – The Cavachon

"Aside from being the ULTIMATE family dog: Cavachons are funny, super sweet, loyal, smart, very tolerant, willing to please, and they forever look like a puppy!"

__Linda Kaiser__

www.smoochmypups.com

The Cavachon is a what is known as a designer dog, a label that it shares with the incredibly popular Labradoodle and Goldendoodle. It also has a remarkably short history, and because it is not a purebred, you cannot enter it into any dog show. However, during the relatively short history of this breed, the Cavachon has made a phenomenal impression people on who love dogs. This breed tends to combine the best aspects of their equally lovable parents, the Cavalier King Charles Spaniel and Bichon Frise.

However, because this breed does not have an extensive history like the two breeds from which the Cavachon originates, it is wise to have a better idea of the characteristics of the two parent breeds too. If you are considering getting a Cavachon, knowing the typical characteristics of the parents will give you an idea of what to expect.

Descriptions and Defining Characteristics

Since they are not a well-established breed, Cavachons come in a wide range of looks. Sometimes they favor the Cavalier King Charles Spaniel, other times they favor the Bichon Frise. There are a few things about them that are definitive though, because both of the original breeds have similar features.

Appearance

Cavachons are never going to be medium or large dogs. You can expect your adorable bundle to be between 13 and 20 pounds as an adult and will be roughly a foot tall. Their fur is typically soft and silky, but coloring is where their appearance really starts to differ. Your Cavachon can have a coat in any one of several different colors:

- White
- White and black
- Black
- Black and tan
- Apricot
- Tricolored

With such a variety of colors, they can be incredibly difficult to identify when they are young. One nice thing is that they are typically low-shedding dogs, and if they get the majority of their grooming genetics from the Bichon Frise side, they will be hypoallergenic.

Temperament

Another near universality of the Cavachon is that it is an incredibly friendly and loving dog. While many smaller dogs tend to be either scared of children or a bit annoyed with them, Cavachons love kids. Children offer them the chance to get some of their energy out and get the attention they crave. Cavachons tend to love people and just want to be loved in return. They feel compelled to please people, making them very easy to train. Positive reinforcement works well, with attention being far more effective since they want to make their people happy.

They might bark at people they don't know, but Cavachons don't tend to be a very vocal dog otherwise, making them a very poor guard dog. Even if they were big barkers, they are more likely to try to befriend intruders than terrify them. Their adorable appearance, even as adults, also makes them less than intimidating.

They tend to be a relatively easy-going breed, making them great for apartments. You will need to take your Cavachon out for several walks a day as they do have energy, but they will be happy on rainy days if you want to spend time playing with them indoors.

Defining the Cavalier King Charles Spaniel Characteristics

Providing half of the parentage of the Cavachon, the Cavalier King Charles Spaniel is another dog with a relatively short history, but with origins that are incredibly long. At the core, the Cavalier King Charles Spaniel is a small dog with many of the spaniel traits. Small spaniels became popular during the 16th and 17th centuries; this breed was named after King Charles II. When they fell out of popularity, the breed largely died out. It was brought back following WWI and gained in popularity over the 20th century.

It is a perfect combination for a fun-loving dog that will be adored by the family.

Appearance

Often described as beautiful, the Cavalier King Charles Spaniel, also called the Cavie, is without a doubt an attractive dog. With a long sleek coat that comes in a range of colors, this breed looks regal. There are four primary Cavie colors:

- Tricolor with black markings dotting the white base and tan around the face
- Blenheim, or a chestnut color on a white base
- Tan spotting a black base coat
- A solid reddish-brown

One of the most desirable characteristics of the breed appearance is that its tail moves as it walks, creating a slightly hypnotic effect. With large, dark, round eyes perfectly centered between long elegant looking ears, a slight tilt of the Cavie's head and you will pretty much do whatever the dog wants.

The long coat does shed, and it sheds a lot. This is one reason why not all Cavachons are hypoallergenic. If they have dominant Cavie traits, they may shed more than others that have a majority of Bichon Frise genetics.

Cavalier King Charles Spaniel

Height and weight

The larger of the two breeds, the Cavalier King Charles Spaniel only reaches about 1 foot in height up to the shoulder. Weighing between 13 and 18 pounds, this breed is one that is easy to take with you when you travel and to rest in your lap. Given their size, they are easy to walk and manage, which is good considering they are a more energetic dog. With such an adorable face, you have to keep your sharing of food to a minimum as the breed can quickly gain weight if constantly given people food. This definitely takes willpower, but if you do give your Cavie people food from time to time, make sure to follow it up with a nice, long, tiring walk.

Cavalier King Charles Spaniel

Temperament

The Cavie is a particularly loving dog, to the point of being more dependent. This means that they do not like to be left alone. They love people and are not afraid to say hello to pretty much anyone, making them a very poor guard dog. Always looking for a lap, Cavies want to be part of the action and attention.

With their spaniel background, they do tend to have moderate to high-moderate energy levels. Some may want to chase smaller animals, which should be easy to manage and train out of them with positive reinforcement.

They are sometimes used as therapy dogs because of their very friendly nature and eagerness to be with people. Since they love to be with people, they are a great breed for helping people.

Defining the Bichon Frise Characteristics

The Bichon Frise is a descendant of the Water Spaniel, bred specifically to bring out the charming appearance associated with the breed. The origins are not entirely known because the breed so old that there is very little documentation on it. However, it is known that both the Spanish and French who encountered the dog fell in love with it and brought it back to their countries. In addition to the cuddly appearance, the Bichon Frise has always been a relatively mild-mannered dog, which is somewhat unique for a dog of smaller stature. The dog gained popularity during the Renaissance and was often the subject of the artwork of Francisco Goya, a famous painter and printmaker. It has been an incredibly popular breed for a long time, being a very fun-loving dog that can easily capture anyone's heart.

Appearance

The other half of the Cavachon parentage, the Bichon Frise's most obvious characteristics are right there in the breed's name – Bichon Frise is French for "fluffy white dog." They are an incredibly adorable breed. They look like walking fluff balls with stuffed animal-like round eyes and a cute button nose. Most people immediately want to pick up a Bichon Frise and hug it like a teddy bear because of how otherworldly adorable they are.

Bichon Frise

Their amazingly fuzzy coats are similar to the poodles in appearance, and it is equally hypoallergenic. This has made them increasingly popular as they require little grooming (beyond washing their white coats clean after a bout out in the mud) and are easy to have around even for those with allergies.

Height & weight

Slightly smaller than the Cavie, most Bichon Frises don't even reach a foot tall to their shoulders, reaching only between 9 and 11 inches. Their incredibly fluffy appearance hides their very little frame, only weighing about 7 to 12 pounds. Despite their small stature and stuffed animal likeness, they are not classified as a toy breed. Their cute appearance can make you more inclined to share your food, but you should avoid it as they cannot care a lot of extra weight on their small frames and stay healthy.

Temperament

An incredibly loving, low-key dog, it is easy to see what has made this breed so popular for so long. They are fairly energetic; but with their small stature, a few medium-length walks and a vigorous play session or two will be more than enough to keep them fit. They are very intelligent, and because they love to make people happy, Bichons aren't usually destructive. Make sure to train them to keep their active minds and bodies happy, as well as for building some very strong bonds from the beginning.

They are also used as therapy dogs. In addition to their fantastic personality and desire to please, the fact that they don't shed much makes them perfect for working as therapy dogs.

CHAPTER 2
Breed History and Characteristics

*"Because they are a hybrid from two breeds with different charac-
teristics, there is no stereotype for Cavachons. Some look more like their
Spaniel parent, others look more like their Bichon Frise parent, while
many are a middle of the road mix of the two. Despite their differences in their appearance, they do generally share a sweet, people friendly,
non-aggressive temperament which is characteristic of both the parent
breeds."*

Sandy Wasicek

www.bichonpups.com

The Cavachon is an incredibly new breed, so much so that calling
it a "breed "is almost a misnomer. Most Cavachons are still bred
from parents of two different breeds (the Cavie and Bichon), not from two
parents who are both Cavachons. Both of these parents have lengthy, in-
triguing histories that are well worth looking into if you do not want to
deal with the kinds of uncertainty that comes with a designer dog.

However, given the similar natures of both the Cavie and the Bichon,
the traits of the Cavachon are still fairly predictable. It has been why the
dog has become so popular during its short history.

A Short History

The decade when the Cavachon first started being bred more frequently is up for debate. Given how much positive publicity both of
the original breeds have gotten throughout their histories, it is easy to
imagine that the Cavachon actually started much earlier, just not necessarily intentionally so. The earliest known intentional breeding began
around the late 1960s in Iowa. The first larger operation began around
the 1990s, and it appears that was when the designer breed was first
called the Cavachon .

About Designer Dogs

Given its brief history and being a mixed breed, the Cavachon is not recognized by the American Kennel Club. No designer dog is recognized by this well-known club. Since many designer dogs are bred for looks alone, the American Kennel Club pushes for pure breeds with longer histories and established temperaments, particularly those that have declined in numbers, such as Otterhounds. They argue that creating new breeds is unnecessary because humans have already established the same traits through breeding over centuries. It is the well-defined personalities and traits of the purebred dogs that they argue make them a better choice than a designer dog.

The American Kennel Club's concerns are certainly legitimate, particularly with puppy mills that seek to make a quick profit from designer dog trends. Before selecting a breeder, take the time to do your research. You want to find a breeder who knows the parents well and takes very good care of them. You want to find a breeder who can tell you about the parents, their personalities, and their parentage. For designer dogs, you want to find breeders who love dogs and know how to breed them right, not people who are simply trying to make a lot of money off of the trend.

Photo Courtesy of
Adam Ball

*Photo Courtesy of
Melissa Haskell*

Unpredictable Traits

The American Kennel Club's assertion that designer dogs' traits are more difficult to predict is true, even for Cavachons. There are many similarities between the Cavie and Bichon, but there are enough differences that you may not necessarily know what health problems or specific personality traits your Cavachon will have.

The traits that overlap between Cavies and Bichons make it easy to have a relatively accurate idea of the primary traits. Your Cavachon is going to be around a foot tall up to the shoulders and will be no more than 30 pounds, and that is if one of the parents is particularly large for the breed. And your cute little dog is going to be incredibly loving because both of the parent breeds are rather dependent and love to be with people.

The basics about your Cavachon are easy to predict, but the other aspects that may vary based on which parent the pup takes after.

If your dog takes after the Cavie, it is likely your pup will want to chase smaller animals, something you will need to train them not to do, especially if you have smaller animals in your home. They have higher energy levels, which means more exercise. If the Cavachon's coat is closer to the Cavie's coat, your dog will shed more than a Cavachon that takes after the Bichon side. The dog probably will shed more, and if you have allergies, you may find that you have a mild reaction.

If your dog takes after the Bichon, your dog will probably be a bit smarter, which means easier overall training. Fortunately (or not, depending on if you keep the right diet for your dog), your dog will be a bit lazier and will likely be okay with longer periods alone.

However, notice that these are really details about the personality, not the overall personality of your Cavachon. The Cavachon is going to be an adorable and companionable dog. Both parents are well-known for being friendly and lovable, making them great therapy dogs. With proper training, you can make sure that any traits you don't want, such as excessive barking or attempting to chase small animals, are not exhibited in your dog. Ultimately, training and lots of love are the best way to make sure your Cavachon is the perfect companion for you and your family. Most of the traits are already there, you just need to encourage them through positive reinforcement. This is why training your young Cavachon is so important.

CHAPTER 3
The Ideal Home

With their compact bodies, the Cavachon can feel at home in nearly any environment, including studio apartments (as long as you train them not to bark too much at noises the neighbors make). Given how loving and dependent they tend to be, there are definitely some environments that are better than others. If you have a small space or no yard, you do need to be aware of your dog's needs to get exercise.

The Cavachon isn't nearly as energetic as some of the other little dogs, but it still has spaniel genetics, which makes it more active than most small dogs . Fortunately, it is incredibly easy to address their exercise needs since they are so small. They are intelligent, but typically not destructively so. With consistent training, you can easily work out any habits of gnawing on furniture and other items that your Cavachon should not be eating. Regular exercise will also go a long way to keep your Cavachon from wanting to chew on things.

Best Environment

Cavachons are growing in demand because of their size, adorableness, and personality. Since they are easy to train, people are frequently left with the impression that they are a nearly perfect dog for those who want a cute little bundle as a companion. This impression is largely accurate, but it is also true that there are some environments that are better for this breed than others.

A compact canine who loves being a lap dog

As an incredibly easy companion, the Cavachon pretty much does well in any environment where they have at least one companion all day. The Cavie genetics makes them predisposed to being dependent, and they do not like to be left home alone for long periods over the course of the day. For people who work incredibly long hours, the Cavachon may not be the best fit because this alone can have a negative effect on them. They love to be with their people; if left with only themselves, Cavachons will not be very happy.

Cavachons pretty much want to spend all day, every day with their people. Of course, there will be times where they are left without peo-

*Photo Courtesy of
Dorren Bowen*

ple, but you should have another pet to keep them company or keep the stints away from home short. For example, if you can go to work later and your child comes home from school a few hours after you leave, this should not be too difficult for your Cavachon to manage. Most Cavachons love sleeping, and their preferred bed is a person's lap.

Alternatively, if you are allowed to take your dog with you or your Cavachon is a therapy dog, their small stature and generally quiet nature makes it easy to take them nearly anywhere. If you are allowed to take your dog to work (probably best not to take a puppy, particularly if they are not house trained yet), this is one very easy breed to take to the office, and your dog will not want for attention since people will be drawn to play with your dog.

The bottom line – your Cavachon is going to want to be with you all of the time. Aggression towards people and most animals are simply not in this dog's nature. The only exception to this are small animals that it may see out on a walk or in the home. If the Cavie genetics are dominant, there may be a desire to chase and hunt.

Even no yard is fine – as long as your cavachon gets moderate exercise

It can be very easy to think that your Cavachon does not need or desire more exercise because your Cavachon is going to be happy to be with you no matter what. Because they are small, they do not require as much exercise as larger dogs, but they do need regular exercise. Yards and large homes are unnecessary as long as your dog gets a solid 30 minutes of running around and playing every day. Several walks over the course of the day can help keep your dog active for longer as well.

If you are not able to go out walking regularly, having a yard will come in handy because your Cavachon will have the space needed to run around. You can go out and lounge while throwing a toy for your Cavachon to fetch. As long as your train your dog, it can be an easy and fun game at the end of the day. You can also take your pup to a dog park to run around a couple of times a week, and that will provide a large portion of the exercise for the day.

Can be very vocal, but not a good guard dog

Your Cavachon may or may not be a vocal dog, depending on which parent they take after. Of course, training your Cavachon not to be too vocal is an option, but you may consider wanting to have them bark at strange noises as a form of extra security for your home.

If your Cavachon is more inclined to barking, be aware that does not translate to ferocity. They do not have a particularly threatening bark, and they definitely aren't an aggressive dog. When they bark at people walking past, it is more of a way of saying hello. If someone tries to break into your home, your Cavachon is much more likely to greet them and try to play than do anything that will make a person feel intimidated.

The cute, little Cavachon is many things, but a guard dog is definitely not one of them.

Floor surfaces

Smooth surfaces can prove to be a bit of a challenge for your Cavachon. While they are small, smooth floors can make them easily lose traction or balance when they get excited and start running around. Hardwood, tile, and vinyl are tricky for any dog and can be a potential hazard when a dog gets too excited. Though it may seem funny, it is not good for your dog's health in the long run to be dashing off across the floor and slamming into walls and doors because they cannot stop themselves.

Putting down carpeting or adding a non-skid throw rug in these areas can make walking around the house safer for your Cavachon.

Nearly perfect family pet

The Cavachon is a nearly perfect breed for any family. They love kids and other animals, so incorporating them into your family is not going to be particularly tricky. Even if you adopt an older Cavachon, as long as you introduce them in a quiet environment, they are likely to acclimate quickly. This dog just loves to be with people, and they are often described as never knowing a stranger. They tend to be patient with younger children, so you will want to monitor them until they are comfortable and your child learns how to be gentle. Once they are, they can be a perfect companion for children young and old. You do want to make sure your small children know to be careful with them because they are not a large dog and you don't want them to accidentally hurt your pup.

Ideal Lifestyle

The most defining personality trait of the Cavachon is how much they love people and that they adore being with their family. It is incredibly easy to bond with them because they just want to please you. As soon as you start to bond, you will have a little shadow following you around the house until you sit. Upon sitting, you will have a leg warmer in your lap.

They do require some exercise, but as long as you aren't feeding them too much or giving them a lot of human food, 30 minutes of vigorous exercise and a few walks should be more than adequate for your pup. If you notice your Cavachon taking an interest in small animals and wanting to chase them, you are probably going to need to give that pup a bit more exercise because they have more of the energetic spaniel genetics.

Strengths

With their adorable large, round, dark eyes, it is so easy to feel like your dog understands you. They are attentive to a remarkable degree that leaves you feeling like the center of their very small, cuddly universe. In addition to typically being an intelligent dog, their desire to please you makes it easy to train them. As long as you train them, you are not likely to have much trouble - the Cavachon is not a headstrong or strong-willed dog (unlike a number of other small dogs, such as the Corgi).

They love to play and have your attention. When you aren't playing with them, they are more than happy to just cuddle up next to or on top of you as a substitute to having your attention. The Cavachon is pretty easy to tire out because of their size. They are not great jogging partners because their stride is a lot smaller than a human's. After you finish a jog though, you can plop down and play with your canine while resting up. Games like fetch and tug of war are more than enough to keep them happily occupied.

If you want to increase your daily steps, the Cavachon is a great addition to the family. You and your spouse, or the entire family, can make some time to take your dog out for a group walk in the evening and a few times over the weekend. The dog will love the time with the full family, and you will have an opportunity to talk with loved ones without overexerting yourself.

Pleasers – plan to train

Training is incredibly important for Cavachon. This means being consistent in your approach. You aren't going to need to be firm or establish an alpha relationship with most Cavachon, but you do need consistency. They are intelligent, so if you aren't consistent, they are likely to take advantage of that.

Training the Cavachon is relatively easy because they really, really love positive reinforcement. Given their size, this is a great piece of news because you don't want to use treats too often. Praise and playtime are some of the best ways of getting your Cavachon to learn a wide range of tricks and behaviors. If you don't train them, they may suffer from the

*Photo Courtesy of
Adam Ball*

same kinds of negative behavior common in little dogs because they are not discouraged from it. Since they are so easy to train, it is well worth the time and you will probably start seeing results a lot sooner than you would with other breeds.

However, this does not mean that you should plan to leave them home alone for long periods of time. Even though they are quick learners, if left alone, they can experience separation anxiety. Having another dog in the family can help mitigate that, as well as acting as another instructor for your Cavachon.

Hypoallergenic

In addition to being incredibly loving dogs, Cavachons are popular because they are considered hypoallergenic. Many of them shed very little (at least those that take after the Bichon), and even people who suffer from allergies are likely to find that they can interact with their Cavachon without medication or constant sneezing. Like the Labradoodle and Goldendoodle, this designer dog has incredibly easy coat maintenance that makes them a fantastic addition to any home. They won't be covering your furniture and all corners of your home with dog hair either, which means that you are not going to see a significant rise in cleaning once you bring your sweet pup home.

This doesn't mean you are completely off the hook for cleaning and brushing your dog. You just aren't going to need to spend time every single day keeping the shedding to a minimum the way you would with most other breeds. Regular brushing is required to keep your Cavachon from getting matted hair, but you won't have to worry about as much dog hair around your home.

A Little Dog for Those Who Love Cuddling and Playing

The Cavachon is bred to be a loving, cuddly dog that can make anyone feel better. They want to spend all of their time with you, either playing and sleeping. When you want to go outside, they are game for it. If it is raining and you just want to sit around, that is fine with them too. They are the perfect friend because what they really want is to be with you. That means whatever you want to do is perfectly fine by them.

Do be prepared for them to want to constantly be with you. Being alone is pretty much a thing of the past once a Cavachon is in your home, but with the right training, that can be perfect. If you train them not to bark much, they will be perfectly happy just lounging and walking with you without making too much noise.

When you have company, they will be just as excited to welcome your company as you. Typically, you won't have to worry about them being aggressive with anyone (although you do need to make sure young children aren't too rough with them). Any dogs already in your home will be just as exciting and enjoyable as the people in your home. This kind of dog is just full of love and attention, and really all they ask is that you be there with them. It is what has made them so popular and lovable.

CHAPTER 4
Finding Your Cavachon

"Find a breeder who instills and nourishes confidence in 'the' puppy during the eight weeks your puppy is still with the breeder. You cannot replace confidence once it is lost. This confidence gives the puppy a good platform for predicting the world around them. A confident puppy is a happy puppy and is especially more trainable."

Melanie McCarthy

www.cavachonsfromthemonarchy.com

By this point, you are probably incredibly excited about finding your new Cavachon. From having fun outside in the backyard or hiking in spring and summer to cuddling up in late fall and winter, you can already imagine just how easy it will be to make your new family member an incredible addition. The possibilities and adventures you can have seem endless. And with such a sweet disposition, it is easy to look forward to having someone excited when you get home. Cavachons are incredibly easy to assimilate into families because they adore people as much as people adore them.

You now have the basic information you need to start looking for your newest family member. It is time to learn how to find that family member, starting with the first question – do you want to bring a puppy into the home, or would you prefer an older dog?

Each Cavachon is different, but they have a relatively predictable personality. They aren't known for being destructive, even though they are an intelligent dog. They aren't particularly energetic, but they are always ready to play. Essentially, your Cavachon is going to want to be with you all of the time but won't require constant play or attention – as long as it can snuggle up next to you wherever you are and whatever you are doing.

There are some things to consider about the Cavachon as a designer dog. If you plan to bring a puppy into your home, you should be wary of puppy mills. You also need to understand how important it is to have regular checkups for your dog. Unlike more established breeds, the Cavachon's health is less certain in that it could have health problems that are prevalent in either of the two breeds that make them. Few Cavachons are born from Cavachons; rather, they are bred from a parent King Charles Spaniel and a parent Bichon Frise. This makes health concerns less predictable and vet visits essential over the Cavachon's entire life.

Adopting From a Breeder

If you have decided on a puppy, there are a lot of considerations you need to work through before you select your puppy. You want a happy, healthy Cavachon. This is likely to be more difficult than you think because many puppy mills try to cash in on popular designer dogs and give no consideration to the health needs of the puppies. Finding a reputable breeder is only the first of several steps in finding your newest family member.

Finding a breeder

There are a lot of breeders for the Cavachon because it is currently a popular dog; however, they are not all equal. For the sake of your puppy, you need to find a responsible breeder who takes the health of both the parents and the puppies seriously. Currently, there are few certified Cavachon breeders because they are a relatively new dog. With the recent boom in popularity, puppy mills and other people are looking to use that to gain a quick profit from the trend. This is why you need to be careful when you select your breeder.

Start by looking for the few certified breeders. Find out the timeline for getting your puppy and determine if it is right for your family. If you find that the wait is too long, you can turn to looking at non-certified breeders, but you will need to ask them many questions to ensure the dogs are treated well and that health issues are taken into account before breeding. Call and ask them the following questions to get an idea of the history of the parents – be prepared for each call to take at least an hour because you need as many details as you can get about the parents before you decide on a breeder. If the breeder is not willing to take the time to answer all of your questions, cross them off of your list of breeders you are considering.

- Can you visit the property to take a look at the parents? If the immediate answer is no, then do not bother to continue. Even if you do not intend to go to the location, the breeders should be willing to let potential puppy parents check out the parents of the puppy. The only exception is if the breeders keep regular blogs and camera footage that you can review. You need to be able to see the conditions and environment of the puppies, and you want to see the parents to make sure they are treated well.

- Ask about health tests and certifications for the parents. Breeders need to have all of the tests and certifications for the parents to ensure that you receive the healthiest puppy possible. Good breeders will often have guarantees against the worst genetic issues. If the breeder is not offering this, do not continue.

- Breeders should take care of all the basics for the puppies, such as their initial vaccines and deworming. It is essential for puppies to have these taken care of when they are six weeks old (too early for them to leave their mother), and you will be responsible for continuing them. After the shots and deworming are started, they need to be continued every three weeks afterward, which means they ought to be well into their shots before the puppy comes to your home.

- Find out what happens during the first phase of the puppies' life - how the breeder takes care of the puppies during the earliest stage of their lives. This will help you know how much work you have to do as well. You will want to keep a consistent training with the dog, and that will be much easier if you continue where the breeder left off. The breeder may also have begun different types of training, such as house and crate training. You will need to know that before getting your puppy home.

- Ask for their advice on raising a Cavachon. A good breeder can make recommendations and will give you options on how to handle some of the less enjoyable phases, as well as things that your puppy is likely to love. A great breeder will also be there to answer questions about your Cavachon long after your dog has reached maturity. They are interested in the dog's well-being and are willing to answer questions over the Cavachon's entire lifespan.

- Ask if they breed F1 Cavachons, or first generation of Cavachon. This means that the breeder only works with one parent who is a King Charles Spaniel and one parent who is a Bichon Frise. They do not breed with Cavachon, only with the two original breeds.

- Get details about the parents, such as their age, weight, size, how many litters they have had, how many puppies they usually have in a litter, and their health. See if you can get current pictures of the parents and their previous puppies to help you know kind of what your puppy will look like.

Photo Courtesy of
Jenna Lovatt

Health tests and certifications

Cavachons tend to be incredibly healthy dogs, and without an extensive history, there really aren't any defined health tests for them. However, you can verify the health tests and certifications that were done for the parents.

- The Cavalier King Charles Spaniel should be cleared of syringomyelia and mitral valve disease.
- Check to see if the parents have been tested for patellar luxation and Legg-Calve-Perthes disease.

Contracts and guarantees

Even though the Cavachon is not a well-established breed, good breeders still offer guarantees for their puppies. This shows that they are confident that the parents are not passing diseases or hereditary conditions on to their puppies that will erode the puppies' quality of life.

Photo Courtesy of Robin Floyd

Contracts and guarantees come with information on the health of the puppy and any recommendations for the new puppy parent to take care of the puppy's health. For example, it may recommend a vet visit within a couple of days of the puppy entering the new home. The puppy will be tested for possible issues so that you can take appropriate steps to minimize or eliminate those issues, ensuring that the puppy grows up to be healthy. If a major health issue is found, the guarantee requires that you bring the puppy back to the breeder. This ensures that you get a healthy dog.

Contracts and guarantees can be incredibly long . Still, you will need to read it in full to ensure that you know what you are contractually required to do and what the breeder is contractually obligated to provide.

Puppy genetics – the parents

Designer breeds like the Cavachon are far less predictable in their health. Pretty much the only way to know what your puppy will look like and how healthy it will be is to learn about the parents. If the parents are healthy and have been cleared of the hereditary diseases associated with the two breeds, the puppies likely will be healthy and happy.

The parents also help to determine the personality of the puppies. There are many similarities between the King Charles Spaniel and the Bichon Frise, but there are some notable differences. If the puppies tend to take after a King Charles Spaniel that likes to chase little animals, you will need to socialize the puppy early to not chase your cat or harass the wildlife in your backyard. If the puppy takes after a particularly vocal Bichon Frise parent, you are going to want to train the puppy to be less noisy.

Selecting your puppy

Selecting a puppy is pretty much the same once you have determined the breed you want – and the Cavachon is no different. You want to find a dog that has the kind of personality that you want. Unlike many other breeds, you pretty much know the primary personality traits, making it relatively safe to select your puppy without having to worry that your dog will have any unexpected surprises in terms of personality.

Watch how the puppies interact with each other – decide if you want the one that is lively and bouncy or the mellower puppy. The ones that interact more with each other can indicate how well the puppy will interact with your current pets.

Watch the overall interaction of all the puppies as well. If it seems like a majority of them are more hyper or aggressive, then you may want to

Photo Courtesy of Benjamin Emmott

wait for another litter. This is typically not a problem with the Cavachon, but it is an example of the kind of group behavior to watch for. Similarly, you want to avoid litters where the puppies seem generally scared and skittish. You will want to make sure the puppies have healthy interactions to ensure that your puppy is not likely to exhibit behaviors that will make training more difficult or socializing a challenge.

Then pay attention to the individual puppies to determine which one you think will work best with your family. The puppies that are very outgoing may be more demanding of attention in the home, while the ones who hang back could be lower maintenance. If all of the puppies pile forward to meet you (which is pretty likely with a Cavachon litter), figure out which one you feel you could bond with the fastest.

When you are picking the puppy, look for the one that exhibits the personality traits that you want in your Cavachon. If you want a forward, friendly, excitable dog, the first one to greet you may be the one you seek. If you want a dog that will think things through and let others get more attention, this is the mellower dog that may be better for your home.

Beware of puppy mills

As with all designer dogs, you have to be very wary of puppy mills. The parents are often treated poorly and health issues (both acute and genetic) can go largely ignored. This could cause significant problems for the puppies, as potential health issues will be ignored in them as well. Puppy mills don't tend to offer contracts or guarantees, and the puppies likely will not have had all of the necessary medical attention prior to leaving the parents.

Puppy mills have a bad name for a good reason, and many of them are shut down for having poor living conditions for their dogs and puppies. They are only interested in turning the dogs into a quick profit and will do only the bare minimum to care for the puppies. When puppy mills are shut down, the dogs and puppies end up with rescuers.

Adopting an Older Dog

If you do not want to go through all of the necessary training, there are some older Cavachons up for adoption. Because they are a new breed, there are not as many rescues specifically for the Cavachon, but you can still find some Cavachon adults who need a good home.

Benefits

Skipping the puppy phase has many benefits, especially If you don't want to dedicate hours every day to training. You can skip the sleepless nights and accidents in the home, and there are many people who want to start with all that difficult work out of the way. Instead of basic training, you can get right to the good stuff with an adult Cavachon. This is really the appeal of rescuing or adopting an older dog.

Even though they are no longer puppies, Cavachon adults will probably bond with the family relatively quickly because they love people. You will be able to dive right into the kinds of training you want to do and will be able to include the dog in longer walks. They will enjoy all the new stuff you have to show them without wanting to eat the leash while you walk. They have a much better attention span and can pick up on your facial cues to get a better idea of what you want. The older the Cavachon, the better the lap dog too. They love the 30 minutes of walking and the several hours of being a couch potato with you, anything that you want to do will make them happy.

Adult Cavachons are ideal for individuals and families who do not have the time or patience to work with a puppy. You will need to be more careful with older Cavachon if you have pets because if they were not properly socialized, there may be some initial tension in your home.

Rescues

There are not many Cavachon rescues because it is a designer dog. A large portion of the Cavachons currently in shelters and rescue systems are the result of puppy mills that were shut down for poor breeding practices and unhealthy environmental conditions. This does not mean that there is definitely something wrong with the dog.

You can look around your area for local rescues that specialize in Cavachons. Make sure to set aside time to visit the rescue facility to see what kinds of conditions the dogs are living in before you make your selection. You should also ask about references or read reviews online to see what kind of experience you are likely to have with the rescue. This is true if you go to a shelter as well.

Most shelters and rescues will establish requirements for your dog because they want to find the right forever home for their dogs. Once a dog leaves, they want to make sure that the dog is treated well and does not end up back at the shelter needing a new home. You are not likely to have any information on the health or personality of the parents, which means vet visits are going to be critical for your Cavachon. Shelters and rescues do some of this but typically cannot complete a full battery of tests that can help you understand any potential health issues. This means you are going to need to plan to spend a bit more money to ensure the health of your dog, but you aren't going to need to keep returning to the vet like you would with a puppy.

Introducing an older cavachon to children and other pets

Adult Cavachons are already trained to a certain point, and you can train them further if you have certain behaviors you don't like. However, if they were not socialized when they were young, they may not be as patient with children and other pets. You will want to know the adult Cavachon's history with small animals and children before bringing your new dog home to them. If there is no certainty that the dog has been ex-posed to either, you will need to be extra careful about the introductions.

Cavachons aren't aggressive or territorial, but children and other pets can be a unique challenge for a Cavachon who has not lived with them. Make sure your child understands that there will be no playing with the dog without adult supervision during the first week at the very least. You will probably want to keep play supervised for the first month to make sure your dog is adjusting to the new environment. Your Cavachon will be more accepting of the children and other pets once they feel safe. They are people pleasers, but you want to make sure there is no unnecessary stress on them as they are getting familiar with their new environment.

CHAPTER 5
Preparing for Your Puppy

"Cavachons make fabulous therapy dogs, for all ages. They can support anyone with additional needs, who is looking for a loyal loving friend."

Jenna Lovatt

www.pawfectcavachons.co.uk

The arrival of your Cavachon puppy is undoubtedly something you are looking forward to with eager anticipation. Whether you have been waiting for your puppy to get old enough to leave momma dog or are planning to bring a rescue dog home, you have probably been getting excited for a while. One of the best ways to get you through during this period of waiting is by taking care of everything you have to do before you pup comes home. Even if you are getting a Cavachon that is a few years old, there are a couple of days' worth of preparation. It is typically best to spread out what you need to do over several days so that you aren't rushed or miss something. Cavachon puppies in particular need to have a home that is secured so that they don't hurt themselves trying to stay with you.

Preparing Your Kids

The first place to start with preparation is with your kids. Cavachons love people, even young children. However, they are a small dog and you will want to make sure that your child interacts with them in a way that does not hurt your Cavachon. Your kids are probably going to spend more time with your new dog than you are, and you want to make sure that they know how to behave. As soon as your Cavachon puppy arrives, your kids are going to be too excited to try to learn anything new. That means they have to already know the best way to interact with the family's new addition before you bring the new puppy home.

Establish rules and frequently ask your kids about different scenarios to ensure they know what they should do. That way, when your

Cavachon enters the home, you can monitor them, and if they are too excited, you can simply ask them a question that they already know how to answer. This will make them quickly start behaving in a way that is more appropriate. Do not leave your Cavachon alone with the children for the first few days to make sure they don't get too excited or rough with playing, especially if you bring home a puppy that hasn't learned how to express unhappiness or pain.

Teach your children these five rules to keep your puppy and children playing in a way that builds a fantastic bond.

1. Be gentle. Cavachon puppies and adults are absolutely adorable, but they are also small and not up for rough play. It is never a good idea to be rough with a puppy or even an adult Cavachon.

    Make sure your children understand the consequences if they play too rough with the new family member. Puppies and dogs that are afraid may growl and nip, so it is important to make sure the kids don't scare the dog. Make sure that your child understands that rough play is not good for the dog to avoid drama.

2. Chase should not be played inside. This is going to be difficult for children to remember because it is so tempting to start running with a Cavachon. They are so cute as their little ears flop while they try to run to catch up, but you do not want your children or dog running through your home. Not only is your puppy (or child) likely to get hurt running in the home, it can create a feeling of insecurity for the Cavachon. Even if your Cavachon feels safe, you don't want the dog running around as an adult – once that behavior is learned, it is difficult to train your dog not to run in the home.

3. Avoid mixing meal time and play time. Your Cavachon should be left alone to eat in peace instead of feeling like the food might be stolen. It is also good for your children to focus on eating their own meals as you do not want them feeding your puppy from their plates. Cavachons are not known for being aggressive, but you don't want the puppy to feel anxious about eating.

4. The puppy should be left on its own feet – it shouldn't be picked up. Young children need to be reminded that puppies are not dolls – they're not there to be constantly picked up and carried. Even if your child is careful, it can be incredibly uncomfortable for the Cavachon puppy to be lifted off the floor. The puppy may be small, but children often cannot provide adequate support for a puppy's back half. This can end up hurting the puppy, particularly the spine. Even older children should not be picking up the puppy because if the puppy nips, the surprising pain could result in dropping the puppy.

The great thing about Cavachons is that there are plenty of games that be played right there on the floor. All they want is attention, and kids have an excuse to crawl around on the floor and see what kinds of games are the most fun. You will need to make sure to follow your own rules – if you are picking up the puppy, your kids will definitely do the same.

5. Anything that is valuable needs to be kept out of reach of both your puppy and your child. Children will grab whatever is in reach and start to play with a new puppy, and they are not going to pay attention to what it is until too late. Being proactive and putting valuable things out of reach can make sure you don't have problems later. It isn't just children either – teenagers are not any more likely to pay attention when there is a puppy in front of them. Stuffed animals, towels, and anything that you don't want to be torn up or dirtied should be out of the areas where any playing occurs.

Photo Courtesy of Alison Kelay

Preparing Your Current Dogs

Preparing your dogs for a new puppy can be a unique challenge. Even if you have introduced a new dog before, there are different considerations you need to make for older dogs; they may not be as accepting of a puppy as when they were younger. Preparing your current dogs will be a lot different than preparing children for a new puppy because your dogs need something entirely different than a set of rules and reminders. Without the pre-puppy talk, you may feel there isn't much you can do, but that isn't true. Here are several tasks you can complete prior to your puppy's arrival to prepare your current pets.

Create a space just for the puppy. For at least the first few days (if not weeks), your puppy should not be interacting with your dogs unless there is an adult around to supervise them. This is true even if you work at home – if you aren't paying attention to the puppy, make sure the puppy is separated from the other dogs. There should not be any belongings of your other dogs in the puppy's space either. If your dog has a favorite chair, make sure the puppy's space does not encroach on that space.

Establish a neutral location for your dog to meet the puppy, such as a park near your home. Your dog needs to meet the puppy in a place where possessive tendencies will not immediately kick in at the meeting. The last thing you want is for your dog to react territorially with your puppy. Having the initial meeting somewhere that is familiar to your dog but that is not within your dog's territory will help make the meeting easier to manage. Once your dog has a chance to sniff and get familiar with the new puppy, it will not be as much of a threat in the home.

Plan to have another adult present at the meeting and make sure you know who will keep the current dog calm during the meeting. It is very like that one or both of the canines will be incredibly excited about the meeting, and it could quickly become too much for one person to handle. The person who runs the home and the other people who will be responsible for taking care of the dog and the puppy should also be present. This will help establish the hierarchy for your puppy, although it is unlikely that it will much matter to your Cavachon. It is best not to have young children at the initial meeting as there will be enough energy and excitement between the dog and the puppy.

Realize that it may take a while for your dog to get acclimated to having a puppy in the home. Even if your dog is more than happy to have the puppy around, it is best to keep them separated for the first week while the puppy learns the rules. Your dog will need some time to adjust to sharing your attention. Once your Cavachon puppy is allowed to enter other areas, your dog is probably going to have a lot less alone time, something that will be tiring for older dogs.

For homes with more than one dog, you will need to follow the same rules, adding one additional adult per dog at the initial meeting. The personality of each dog should be considered prior to the meeting. If possible, try to have the dogs meet the puppy one at a time, with the other dogs either in the vehicle or standing further away, so you can gauge each's reaction to the Cavachon puppy. This will keep the puppy from being overwhelmed and keeps the dogs from being too excited (the excitement of one will be contagious to the rest, making for an incredibly boisterous encounter).

Dangerous Foods

With a dog as friendly and companionable as a Cavachon, you really need to be aware of the foods that they should not eat, as should your children. It is going to be incredibly tempting to give them some of the food you are eating because it is easy to think that a small amount won't do much – however, it will. The Cavachon is not a big dog, and it will not take much of the wrong kinds of food to do serious harm. Most people know not to feed chocolate to dogs (even people who have never had one), but there are several other foods that are far more dangerous.

The following is a list of foods that you need to make sure are never accessible to your adorable little Cavachon.

- Apple seeds
- Chocolate
- Coffee
- Cooked bones (they can tear soft tissue when they splinter in the dog's mouth or stomach)
- Corn on the cob (it is the cob that is deadly to dogs, corn off the cob is fine, but you need to make sure that your dog cannot reach any corn that is still on the cob)
- Grapes/raisins
- Macadamia nuts
- Onions and chives
- Peaches, persimmons, and plums
- Tobacco (your Cavachon will not know that it is not a food and may eat it if left out)
- Xylitol (a sugar substitute in candies and baked goods)
- Yeast

These are foods that could be deadly to your puppy, but there are also foods that your dog shouldn't eat to stay healthy. Check out The Canine Journal list of foods and make sure that your family abides by the rules of your house in terms of what people food your dog is given.

Yes, it is going to be difficult because you will want to share. Even for safe foods, you should keep it to a minimum how much you share, with the recommendation being not to give your dog any human food. Dogs do not have the same metabolism as humans, and the highly processed food is really not good for their systems. To keep your Cavachon healthy, it is best to get the puppy used to eating dog food and keep all of the dangerous foods well out of reach.

Hazards To Fix

Just like you have to babyproof your home for a newborn, you are going to need to spend a good bit of time preparing your home for your Cavachon puppy. There are many potentially dangerous things, some of which you probably don't notice because you do not see the world from the Cavachon's perspective. One thing you should do long before your puppy's arrival is to get down on your stomach in each room and look around for potential dangers. The following sections cover many of the most common potential problems, but every home is unique. Doing your own thorough inspection from your puppy's perspective will help you see the world from an entirely different point of view.

Start your puppy-proofing at least a month before your puppy's arrival. This will give you ample time to take care of everything.

Kitchen and eating areas

The kitchen is always one of the most dangerous areas for animals and children. There are poisons in the cabinets, sharp utensils, and a host of other things on which pets and kids can hurt themselves. Securing your kitchen area will be the same for your Cavachon puppy as it would be for a toddler. They do not tend to be troublemakers. They typically to use their intelligence to make you happy, but that does not mean they won't try to entertain themselves. With all of the smells and food, the kitchen is a curiosity for puppies (and dogs). They will likely work their way into your cabinets if the cabinets are not secured. In addition to keeping hazardous foods out of reach of your puppy, you need to make sure poisons are always stored in a place where your Cavachon cannot get to it. Don't leave buckets with cleaning supplies in them or set cleaning supply bottles on the floor. All your Cavachon has to do is knock them over and spill the contents all over the floor. Get accustomed to storing all of your supplies in the cabinets where they are secure.

You also need to start putting your garbage can in a secure location. There will be a lot of things from the kitchen the end up in it, such as plastics, cooked chicken bones, broken glasses, and wrappers with interesting smells. Even a small Cavachon puppy will look for ways to tip it over and enjoy the contents. Either store your kitchen garbage can in the pantry or under the sink to ensure your puppy cannot get to it.

Make sure there are no cords that will be within reach. Your teething Cavachon pup is likely to want to chew on them and see what happens when they pull on them. This is clearly an electrical danger, but that is not the only risk. When the cords are attached to things like toaster ovens and blenders, this becomes very dangerous because it could crush the little pup. Keep all cords out of reach.

Bathroom and laundry

The next most dangerous room for your puppy will be the bathroom, and it will require the same puppy-proofing that you did in the kitchen. All poisons need to be kept behind locked cabinet doors. Sharp objects need to be in locked drawers (except for the ones that are too high for a small dog to reach). Get used to keeping your toilet closed and avoid using instant cleaners (you are going to need to get used to cleaning the toilets the old-fashioned way). Even if you keep the toilet seat closed, all it takes is a visitor leaving the lid up and your puppy could try to drink from it.

While not quite as dangerous as the kitchen and bathroom, the laundry room does have its share of potential puppy hazards. Laundry detergent and other cleaning supplies that you store in the laundry room need to be out of reach. If you have cabinets, make sure they are locked because they likely serve as storage for other items, and you do not want your puppy getting into them. If possible, find a way to keep clothing off of the floor. You don't want your puppy eating your dirty clothing – or dragging your dirty undergarments around your home. There will also be times when items with potentially dangerous chemicals on them will be put in the dirty laundry, and you do not want those to be in within reach of your Cavachon. The easiest thing to do is to keep the door closed, but you should still make sure things are out of reach. You will likely let the Cavachon follow you into the room and your attention will be elsewhere while the puppy is exploring.

*Photo Courtesy of
June Van Klaveren*

Other rooms

Just like you did in the kitchen, you are going to need to go around and make sure all electrical cords are off of the floor, cleaning products and dangerous items are out of reach, and there is nothing under furniture that could be dangerous to your puppy. This includes pens and pencils, which will likely look like chew toys to your puppy. You do not want them getting sick from the graphite or pen ink, nor will you want to have to clean up the mess.

Fireplaces need to be cleaned and all cleaning supplies stored out of reach, including things like pokers. Make sure that the interior is secured so that your Cavachon cannot enter it.

Have baby gates for stairs to keep your puppy from tumbling down them. It is best in the first months to avoid the stairs with your little puppy. Cavachons as adults are small; their puppies are tiny. To avoid them falling down the stairs, just keep them away from them. You may want to plan to have a training session with any stairs you have inside once your puppy is a bit older.

If you have a cat, make sure the litter box is in a location that your puppy cannot reach. It won't need to be too high off the ground, but it does need to be secured away from your puppy. You will want to make sure your cat has time to learn the new location before the puppy arrives too. The last thing you should do to a cat is change where its restroom is located while it is coping with a new, energetic puppy.

Garage

Garages are a terribly dangerous place for any dog, but especially small puppies. They are going to be able to get into areas that you had not even considered. Under workbenches and cars, in small spaces, and through holes you didn't know where there, puppies will find all of the most dangerous places without even trying.

It is best to keep your Cavachon out of the garage. If your Cavachon does go into the garage, never leave your dog alone in there. Since you will likely be taking your Cavachon through the garage on the occasion, it is best to puppy-proof it too.

Equipment, tools, car parts, and yard supplies all need to be stored off the ground where the puppy cannot reach. Fortunately, that is relatively easy since your Cavachon is not going to get too big. This includes bike tools, leaf blowers, and other equipment that you don't want your Cavachon chewing on if you are hanging out in the garage. Fishing equipment also needs to be organized and stored where your puppy will not eat your bait or get hurt on hooks. Make sure nothing is dangling over any countertops either.

Get down low and look around to see what all is a potential danger to a young dog. Block any small areas where your puppy could potentially crawl, move wires and cables up out of reach, and store chemicals and tools in a place that puppies and children cannot touch.

Outdoors and fencing

Never leave your Cavachon unattended in your yard, even if you have a fence. First, your dog is not going to like being away from everyone. Second, there are far too many dangerous things in the yard for a puppy or young dog.

As long as you never send your Cavachon out alone, it should be relatively easy to puppy-proof the yard. Set aside an hour or two (depending on the yard size) to look it over and make sure the usual hazards are out of reach. Fertilizer, gardening tools, and power tools should all be stored in the garage or shed. Look over the fencing for holes near the ground or places where a puppy may be able to burrow out. This includes looking for breaks that could trap your Cavachon. Also, if there is water in your backyard, such as a pool or small pond, make sure your puppy cannot get to it.

Determine where you want your Cavachon to use the restroom outside. This is going to be incredibly important because it will make the clean-up much easier. Make sure that the location is safe (no holes in the ground that could hurt the puppy and no cleaning supplies). There shouldn't be anything large and potentially dangerous in the area, such as a birdbath. An excited puppy or child may knock them over while playing. Your Cavachon is going to learn really quickly where to go to the bathroom if you stay consistent, and you want to make sure there are no risky items in the area.

Spend time walking around the yard checking it out. You should do this several times over the course of the month, keeping an eye out for anything that needs to be moved or fixed.

Supplies And Tools To Purchase And Prepare

Once the home is secure, it is time to make sure you have everything you need before your Cavachon arrives. Create a checklist of everything you know you will need and anything you think would be beneficial. Even if you don't buy anything extra, there are a lot of items that are basic needs for your puppy. The following list can help you get started:

- Crate
- Bed
- Leash
- Doggie bags for walks
- Collar
- Tags
- Puppy food
- Water and food bowls (sharing a water bowl is usually ok, but your puppy needs his or her own food dish if you have multiple dogs)
- Toothbrush
- Brush
- Toys

Anything else you want for your puppy, add it to the list, such as flea treatments so that you can start treating your dog at the right age.

Training tools and treats should be on that list - you just need to determine which one you want to have for your puppy. A combination of treats and toys will have the best results because you will not want to continually give your puppy food. You will also need to get equipment for training indoors for the first few weeks. Toys will need to be the right fit for your Cavachon puppy's little mouth. Don't get anything too big or heavy. Fortunately, your Cavachon is going to follow you around, making it easy to work training and play time into the day. It will build up your puppy's stamina though, so plan to increase play time to both keep your puppy from boredom and in shape.

Planning the First Year's Budget

While they aren't nearly as expensive as newborn humans, puppies can be relatively costly. Setting up your budget before the puppy arrives will make sure that you can afford the things you need over the course of the year. This will include things like vet visits for shots, training supplies, and food. Make sure to include some cushion room because it always costs more than you expect.

Start the budget as soon as you decide to get a Cavachon. They may not require much extra for their care (you are their favorite source of entertainment, so you aren't going to need to constantly find ways to keep them from boredom), and they are small, but all dogs cost a lot their first year as you learn what they need. You are also going to need to do a good bit of research in finding a vet for your Cavachon. Vets have different prices for different cities and states, and you want one with a great reputation, as well as knowledge about designer breeds. Because they have much shorter histories, the types of typically health problems vary much more for designer breeds than purebred dogs; however, they have an easier history to track than mutts. You want a vet who can address the potential issues common with designer breeds.

Summary

Your Cavachon's focus is pretty much going to be guaranteed around you and your family. They are intelligent, but they do not tend to cause the kinds of problems that Corgis and other intelligent dogs do because Cavachons find all the entertainment they need with their people. This makes them incredibly fun and enjoyable. In those first few months though, they are going to be learning everything, and that means investing more time to keep them safe and happy. To make sure you aren't caught off-guard, make sure you have everything set up well ahead of your Cavachon's arrival.

Make sure that your family, including your pets, are prepared for the new arrival. Have the day of the introduction already planned out, particularly with young kids and dogs. Spend some extra time with your current pets so that they do not feel like they are being replaced. You need to plan to spend extra time with them after the puppy's arrival too because they will feel left out while you are training and playing with the puppy. Take longer walks or plan to spend more time playing in the yard. Make time in your schedule now to do that once the puppy arrives because it will be much harder to work it into your schedule later. Having something familiar will help your dog to adjust faster to the little puppy.

CHAPTER 6
The First Week

As soon as your Cavachon steps foot in your home, everything is going to be different. Bringing your new family member home is going to consume your time and attention, but you probably won't mind at all because of how adorable your puppy is. The time is going to fly as you get to know your Cavachon's personality and interests. Your Cavachon's abilities will also reflect the time and effort you put into the training, and it requires a commitment on your part to make sure you Cavachon remains happy and healthy.

That first week will establish a lot about your relationship and the way your puppy feels about your home. All of the hard work is done (puppy-proofing a home is definitely hard work), and now you get to see that pay off. However, you are going to need to train every day, which could be a bit more difficult when things get busy. No matter how busy you are, make the time to do it so that your puppy doesn't get into trouble as an adult for doing the things you thought were cute when they were small.

Preparation and Planning

As you read in the last chapter, planning and preparation begin long before your pup's arrival. Everything needs to be set up before your Cavachon comes home so that the transition for your family and the Cavachon goes smoothly.

The day before your Cavachon arrives, take time to do a final check of your home. Cavachon puppies are incredibly small, so you should literally get down on your hands and knees and really inspect every room for potential hazards from their angle. This will also help you understand how they see your home.

Have a list of everything your puppy will need right from the start. That list should include the following (this list is not comprehensive):

- Food
- Bed
- Crate
- Toys

- Water and food dishes
- Leash
- Collar
- Treats

Photo Courtesy of Susan Adamson

If you plan to provide a fenced-in area within your home for your puppy, make sure you know how to work the gates and that they are not easy to knock over.

Sit down with the family and make sure everyone understands the rules, particularly children. Proper puppy handling is essential for making sure your children and puppy play well together and that means being strict with your children – not just your puppy. Verify that everyone knows their roles – who will walk the puppy, who will feed and monitor the water bowl, and who will participate in daily training. Training should be everyone's job, but one person should be responsible for the harder tasks on a daily basis, such as training. Others are free to join in, but having a primary trainer who handles it every day helps establish consistency. One adult should be involved with the puppy's training too. Pairing up can help teach children about responsibility, so that is another option. One adult and one child can monitor the water bowl; one adult and child can feed the puppy. This makes it easier to ensure that nothing important is forgotten in the early days.

Finally, your Cavachon is going to need a routine in the early days. It is fine if that schedule changes later on, but in the beginning, a predictable schedule helps the puppy feel safe and secure in the new home. It is fine to occasionally change up the schedule a little, and you can tweak it as your Cavachon get more comfortable. The schedule will help you as much as the puppy too; if you have a routine, you are less likely to forget a task – autopilot can be a beautiful thing when training a puppy.

The final week before your puppy arrives, run through everything one last time. Try to work on the schedule you want to use to train your puppy, from when you get up and need to make time for walking, to when you go to bed. Things will change, but if you are already accustomed to the schedule (if only a little), it will make things easier after you Cavachon comes home.

The Ride Home

As soon as you meet your Cavachon, it is time to start training. Everything that your puppy will learn has a foundation in that first ride in your vehicle on the way home. Of course, with as cute as that puppy is, you are going to want to cuddle them all the way home, but you have got to start being consistent from that first encounter. Your puppy is learning from what you do and say during those early days, and you want the impression to be friendly and consistent. Those large eyes will stare you down, and if you give in and take the puppy out of the crate, things are only going to get harder as that will be the expectation from that moment on. That adorable little face hides an intelligent mind, and if your Cavachon knows that you are weak to the puppy-dog eyes, they are going to use that against you.

It is recommended to have two adults on the trip to pick up the puppy so that one person can give attention to the puppy while the other drives. The Cavachon will likely not be scared, but you want to reassure the puppy after all of the changes it has experienced. The more positive the driving experience is, the more your Cavachon will enjoy car rides in the future.

Make sure the crate is secure in the car so that your Cavachon is not sliding around the back area. You should not be holding the crate either. The puppy should experience minimal jostling to create a positive experience.

Photo Courtesy of Lynsey Long

First Night Frights

That first night is going to be difficult for your Cavachon. It is the first night away from the mother and comfort that the puppy has known, and it is understandable that this will be terrifying. However, there is only so much you can do to make the puppy feel better without undercutting yourself. What you do not want is for your puppy to think that negative behavior will get the desired results. You need to work through those first few nights to teach your puppy that it is not as scary as it seems and that your home is a safe place.

If you have a policy that keeps dogs off of the bed, you definitely cannot be giving in so early. You cannot bring the puppy into your room to sleep on the bed because that will encourage whimpering and whining every night until that action is repeated. It is nearly impossible to convince your Cavachon that they are not allowed on the bed if you allow them to on the first night.

Considering the number of strange noises and smells, your Cavachon is going to feel uncertain in your home. As a result, the puppy is likely to make a lot of noises, including whimpering, and those eyes are going to try to persuade you to relent on whatever rules you wanted to keep. You need to expect this so that you can be strong. Learning to ignore the noises from your puppy – and not looking at your puppy when you hear them – is going to help you train your dog.

Do not move your Cavachon just because you don't want to deal with the noises. If you ignore them long enough, over a few days, they will stop. Moving your puppy away from you will terrify the puppy and prove that the puppy is alone in your home – a fear that you do not want to instill (let alone confirm). Even if your puppy wants more room, keeping the Cavachon in the designated space over the first week will show the dog that it is not alone, but there are rules to follow.

Like having a new baby, you probably are not going to get much sleep in those early days. After all, you do have a small, furry baby to tend to now. It is all part of what you sacrifice to start with a puppy instead of an older dog. Having a designated sleep space for your Cavachon proves that there is space designated just for your dog – even if your Cavachon has no interest in having personal space. There should be boundaries to help the puppy understand the current restrictions. Over time, you will be able to let the puppy wander around the home, but for now, the Cavachon should be kept in an area where the puppy can learn to be comfortable. You are going to need to go into that space often as your puppy is not going to like being alone. Make sure to have another area nearby for the puppy to use the bathroom. If you want to start by training your puppy to only use the restroom outside, you are going to have to get accustomed to sleeping even less, as you will need to take the puppy outside several times during sleep hours.

First Vet Visit

This is definitely something that you and the puppy will both face with trepidation. Yet within the first day or two of the puppy's arrival at your home, you need to go to the vet together for the first time. It is necessary to ensure that your puppy is healthy as well as create that initial bond between the vet and your puppy. Of course, your puppy is not going to be happy, but it is important to get familiar with the vet. As an outgoing, friendly dog, it is very likely that your Cavachon will have a much better relationship with the vet than other breeds.

Photo Courtesy of
Glynis Smith

The vet will conduct the initial assessment and gain a baseline of your puppy's health. This will also help as your Cavachon grows to make sure that the puppy is maturing and developing as expected.

As the first visit, your puppy will probably be pretty excited and want to explore the room. Of course, meeting everyone in the room is also something you are likely to have to contain, especially for older animals that are not interested in being pestered by a puppy. Make sure to ask everyone before letting the puppy approach any other animal in the waiting room. Many of them are likely there for an ailment and may not be feeling well enough to entertain the puppy.

Over the course of the encounter, make sure to give positive feedback for good behavior. Anything your puppy does that you want to be continued should be praised – this will have a much greater effect than any kind of food because your attention and happiness are what your Cavachon wants. This will help your puppy to get more comfortable with the environment so that future visits are not as scary. The positive attention will help associate the vet with a positive environment.

The Start of Training

Training may start when your puppy gets in the car, but you have a lot more work that is more time intensive ahead of you. Not that Cavachons are hard to train, but they can persuade you that you have better things to do than to train them. That cute little face and adorable eyes can easily distract you from what you need your puppy to learn. Over the next few weeks and months, you need to establish some basic training foundations.

Barking

Some Cavachons are prolific barkers, but you can train them out of this habit. They are prone to barking on walks and when they see or hear something outside. Start training your puppy not to bark at random things during that first week. It may mean a few extra treats (make sure to take them on the walk), but that is okay in the early days and will help your puppy to be quieter.

Your Cavachon may also be a bit noisier to get your attention. The best way to discourage this is to ignore your puppy. That does mean you will be training yourself as well as the puppy, so it will likely take time and patience as you figure out when the puppy is barking for your attention or for something else. You can prioritize and start by discouraging random barking first, then stop giving as much attention when the barking is reduced when walking.

The leash

Leash training is going to be a breeze, but keep in mind that it is not exactly natural. Depending on your puppy's personality, the leash may be treated like a chew toy, so you will need to teach the puppy not to do that. For the most part, your puppy is going to be happy just to be included in whatever you are doing. Do be careful not to be too forceful and plan to take short walks in the early day, maybe just around a block. The puppy is going to have a lot sniff and observe, so the walks are not going to be real exercise until the puppy is older.

Teaching respect

Even though the Cavachon is incredibly personable and friendly, you are going to need to teach it to respect the family members. If not trained properly, it could act like a little terror, disregarding family members and barking incessantly. You likely don't need to worry about more serious problems, but you don't want your Cavachon to act like a brat when it gets older – that is simply not cute and gives small dogs a bad image.

Consistency

The best way to gain a Cavachons' respect is through consistency in training. This should be done without inspiring fear – your puppy wants to please you, that is the best leverage for teaching them respect too. They want to have positive attention, so just be consistent in your approach and almost everything else should be easy.

The reason to bring this up is that it is easy to give in to those puppy-dog eyes that the Cavachon will have even as an adult. You will have to be strong, but as long as you are consistent, it really is easy to train most Cavachon.

Acclimation to the home

Any rules you want to enforce will need to be enforced consistently, no matter who the family member is. This means making sure everyone follows the rules. It is easy to think of your Cavachon puppy as an adorable little fluffball, but your puppy is a smart dog, just without many of the usual problems that you would encounter with smart dogs. The one common problem that you do have to watch is being consistent. It will take a while for your puppy to understand that the rules will not change. Being consistent and not bending or breaking of those rules is the best way to get your puppy acclimated to your home.

CHAPTER 7
The First Month

"Separation anxiety can be a concern in the first few months if you do not set clear boundaries from the beginning. A puppy needs time to settle in but also needs rules that the whole family will stick to."

Jenna Lovatt

www.pawfectcavachons.co.uk

When that first week comes to an end, you are going to have a really good idea of what your puppy's personality is like, and it may even be difficult to remember what life was like before the little guy came into your home. You have been learning as much as your Cavachon, and now you have an idea of what works, what doesn't, and how your puppy will try to break the rules.

Training a Cavachon is easy compared to most breeds. The intelligence of the Cavachon means that learning is quick, and the desire to have fun with you is the best incentive a dog can have. They are not known for testing boundaries or being destructive when they are bored. However, that does not mean they are not incredibly intelligent. If there are tricks you want your Cavachon to learn, make sure you plan for it because you may be able to get started as early as that first month.

Not Up to Full Strength

Your Cavachon is never going to be a mass of muscles, but especially as a puppy, your Cavachon is going to be limited in activities. All of that energy and excitement is quickly used up as the puppy explores the house, backyard, and a small portion of the neighborhood. Walks will be short, and you will be staying close to home. Exercise should be broken up over the course of the day because your puppy will not be able to sustain long periods of continuous activity. A few short walks and some energetic play sessions will be more than enough to keep your puppy too tired to get into trouble.

Photo Courtesy of
Susan Adamson

Not only will your puppy require less sustained exercise, there will be a lot of naps mixed into the day, meaning you will have more time to get things done that you need to do. After that short walk, your puppy will be ready to lie down and take a nap, so take that time to do chores and errands. Puppy naps should always take place in the puppy area – no exceptions. If you keep the puppy in a different area, you will have to be ready to drop everything you are doing once the puppy wakes.

After the first month, your Cavachon's energy levels will be obviously higher and the stamina will seem to have doubled. Walks will be longer (although still not a full walk quite yet), and play and training sessions will last longer. This means that you will need to plan to start adjusting your routine to reflect the increased energy and needs of your puppy. You could start taking longer but fewer walks over the course of the day, or make training sessions last 5, 10, or 15 minutes longer.

Setting the Rules and Sticking to Them

One of the biggest problems with intelligent dogs is that failing to be consistent is something they will notice and take advantage of. If you deviate from a schedule or the norm and it is in their favor, they are going to try to keep that going. This is certainly true with Cavachons, which are not only intelligent but also unbelievably adorable. They will use any weakness you have to their advantage.

Fortunately, their idea of taking advantage of you is to get more food from your plate or to stay in bed a little longer. Unlike other intelligent dogs, Cavachons largely focus on getting more time and attention from their people. But you will have to make sure that you stick to established rules so that they are not only happy but healthy too. Don't get in the habit of feeding them from your plate – their little bodies cannot take a lot of this. Enforce training even if your Cavachon does not seem interested. If you act excited, that emotion will quickly transfer.

Your Cavachon needs to know that you are in control. They may not be inclined to acting like an alpha dog, but you don't want them disregarding you either. They will try to convince you that they need more attention, more food, less strict rules, and less work, but you have to teach them that these things are important. It is actually much easier to fall into these traps with a Cavachon than nearly any other dog, which is why you have to make a concerted effort to keep it up. You will quickly feel complacent with everything they have managed to achieve. If you have certain training goals, make sure to stick to them over the course of your Cavachon's training.

Early Socialization

Despite being a very friendly and gregarious dog, your Cavachon's early socialization is still important to make sure they retain this friendliness. With the King Charles Spaniel heritage, Cavachons can be a bit aggressive to smaller animals, which will be a problem on walks. They could also learn to be scared of children and dogs if they are not exposed to them when they are puppies. Socialization is an incredibly important activity that you should focus on during the first few months of your puppy's arrival.

If your family and friends have dogs, ask them to meet up for some puppy playtime. Play dates with dogs you already know will give you a much better environment for keeping control over the situation than a dog park will. Socialization could even be built into your walks if you know enough of the neighbors and their dogs.

Photo Courtesy of
Claire Knox

It is equally important to socialize your puppy with people. This task is easier since people are more predictable in how they react to dogs. With an adorable little Cavachon, this is going to be incredibly easy – just take the puppy out for walks and you are going to get people, particularly children, who want to stop and pet the pooch. You will need to monitor children more closely in their interactions to make sure they are not too rough. Also, let people know that you do not want the puppy picked up. That way the puppy is not accidentally hurt while socializing. Getting hurt will have the opposite effect, as the Cavachon will learn to be wary and fearful of others.

Socialization should be something that you do several times a week, or daily if possible. The more socialized your Cavachon is, the more activities you will be able to enjoy with them later without worrying about how your Cavachon will react.

Do be kind to any older dogs that you encounter. An energetic, little puppy is probably more than they can handle, and you do not want to make them feel uneasy. This is particularly true if you have an older dog in the home. Make sure that your older canine gets some dedicated alone time with you and a lot of time away from the puppy. If your older dog is irritable, you may want to keep the puppy away most to all of the time.

Photo Courtesy of
Kate Harvey

Treats and Rewards vs. Punishments

Treats and training seem to go hand in hand, but with dogs like Cavachons, that is absolutely not necessary. They react just as well to positive rewards as they do to treats. Given how small they are, it is best not to give them much in the way of treats anyway. Since Cavachons are not as food motivated as many other types of dogs, and they are quite intelligent, positive reinforcement is going to be one of the best rewards. Praising your puppy for doing well, providing extra pets and cuddle time, and bringing out new toys will be just as much of a motivator as any treat you can offer. Save the treats for tricks and other unnecessary training that you want to do later.

Exercise – Encouraging Staying Active

Though your Cavachon will not require the same kinds of exercise as many other breeds, they do require at least 30 minutes of solid exercise each day to stay fit. This is important, given how small they are. At this stage, you don't need to worry about 30 minutes at a time, but you should get at least 30 minutes total over the course of the day.

Best Activities

Because they love to be around people, there are a lot of activities that will make your puppy happy. Playing games is best, like running around the backyard and trying to teach your puppy to fetch. As long as there is no running involved, you can play games in the house too, which is great during the summer and winter when your puppy . In addition to no running in the house, make sure that there are no hard toys being thrown. You don't want things to get broken. However, small, light toys can be tossed low to the ground for your little puppy to chase. Keep away is another fun game if there are at least a couple of people available.

Being Careful of the Cold

Cavachons are small and, despite a full coat of fur, do not handle the cold very well. To get the required exercise, make sure that you have some games to play in the house. Never leave your Cavachon outside during the cold months, particularly puppies. They do not have adequate fur to keep them warm, and there is not much fat on their little frames. A designated indoor puppy space should do well during the winter months to keep your puppy safe and warm.

CHAPTER 8
Housetraining

If there is one thing about getting a puppy that everyone dreads, it is the housetraining. The Cavachon makes this tedious and smelly task a little bit less horrid because they want you to please you. They definitely have the brains to keep it from being the miserable experience that it can be with many other breeds. Not that it will be a picnic, it just isn't likely to take as long as you might expect with other dogs.

Before you start, here are a couple of things to keep in mind about training.

1. Cavachon puppies should never be allowed to have free roam of the house. When the puppy is out of the puppy area, the puppy should have constant supervision. That will lower the risk that the puppy will have an accident. Your Cavachon puppy won't want to be in a soiled crate or area either, so this will simplify housetraining.

2. Your puppy needs to have easy access to the locations where you have determined it is okay for the puppy to use the restroom. Having a designated puppy area will help. However, if this is not possible, be prepared for frequent trips outside.

These are two key rules you will have to enforce. To help you be consistent, here are the things you need to consider before your Cavachon puppy arrives.

Understanding Your Dog

Your Cavachon is going to want to stay with you as much as possible – they aren't big on being individuals and do not care to be alone. Still, just because a Cavachon doesn't go to the bathroom outside does not mean that the puppy does not understand that the outdoors is the right place. More likely, the Cavachon is opting for convenience if you aren't consistent. As the human and the adult, you are responsible for not only teaching your puppy what is right, but for also making sure that you provide all of the necessary opportunities to do the right thing.

You can install a doggie door for your Cavachon, although this breed may not be keen on going out alone. You won't need a big door, but it may not be worth the installation if your Cavachon prefers you join to the quick dash outside. You should probably start with taking your Cavachon outside on a leash during the early phases. If you decide to use puppy pads, you need to understand that you will need to move the training outdoors relatively early, as your puppy will learn fast. Puppy pads are a nice transition, but they really should not be used for too long. Leaving puppy pads inside for too long could give your Cavachon the wrong idea that it is alright to go inside.

Small dogs are infamous for being difficult to train, and if you are inconsistent in your approach with a Cavachon, you will find that it could be just as frustrating and headache-inducing as you have heard it can be. Given their intelligence and desire to please, it is your job to provide the opportunities and consistency in the early phases to ensure that your Cavachon learns. Plenty of positive reinforcement will go a long way in making your puppy trainable, and it will make your life easier.

Photo Courtesy of
Sarah Bewick

Inside or Outside

Naturally, you want to train your Cavachon to go outside as soon as possible, but young puppies don't quite understand that in the first few weeks – not until you train them. This could mean that you need to start with indoor training for the short term. This will be especially true if it is cold when your puppy arrives at your home because Cavachons do not do well in the cold. You will need to plan accordingly. If you do start training indoors, make sure your puppy understands that there is only one place where it is okay to go and be consistent with that approach.

If you are able to start training outdoors, you should already have a place chosen for your puppy to go. Now it is time for you to plan frequent (very frequent) trips outside, including at night when you would normally be asleep. It is incredibly time-consuming, but as long as you are consistent in your approach, your Cavachon will start to understand. The first month or so will be rough, but ultimately entirely worth the effort. Though you will need to stay with your Cavachon, your puppy will love it, which will make going outside a great experience. Just make sure to stay positive while you are out there and don't distract your puppy. Having one place for your puppy to go in the yard not only helps to get the idea across that this is the place to use the bathroom, it makes it easier for you to clean up behind your puppy every week. Naturally, you will likely want somewhere close to the door because you don't want your puppy to hold it too long. It is also good to have somewhere close to the door in winter as the Cavachon is going to want to keep restroom outings as short as possible. The poor little guy simply was not built for cold weather.

They Are Pleasures – But You Still Need to Be Consistent

There are so many great things about Cavachons. They are friendly, positive, energetic without being overwhelming, great cuddlers, and potentially quick learners. However, if you fail to be consistent, you are going to find that last aspect to be false, but it isn't the dog's fault - it's yours. Like children, your Cavachon wants to have fun with you and wants you to be happy, but the puppy always doesn't want to do anything that isn't fun. If you let your puppy get away with something once, that sends the wrong message. That does not mean that you should shout at your puppy if an accident happens, but it does mean you need to put more time into getting the puppy outside and focusing on puppy business first.

There will be days where you will want to say that something is good enough, but that is a very dangerous thought process to have with a puppy. They need the rules to always apply, and only strict adherence is good enough.

Also, everyone in the family will need to take the same approach. If you want to use a word to tell your puppy when to use the restroom, everyone in the family will need to use that word. If you plan to take the puppy outside once an hour during the day and several times at night, you or a member of your family will need to do it at the same time daily. If there is a single area in the yard, everyone in the family needs to take the puppy there. This kind of consistency can make the training go smoother.

Positive Reinforcement − It's about Respect

After the puppy uses the restroom, you can either give a treat or play with the puppy a little. The treat will be nice, but you should use it sparingly. Little dogs can get overweight very quickly. With a Cavachon puppy, the playtime will actually be more of a reward than the treat. If that puppy knows that a certain action will mean more playtime, there are very good odds that your puppy will be entirely eager to use the restroom (though it may take a while to understand that she should only do that outside). The puppy will begin to look up to you because it will be obvious that you are in charge. It is a type of respect, although not the kind that you get with working dogs. For the Cavachon, it is more about playing and being with you, and if the puppy knows that something makes you unhappy or upset, avoiding that is a pretty good incentive.

Consistency is obviously required for your Cavachon to understand the rules. They are smart, but not quite as intelligent as a Corgi or a working dog. Cavachons aren't driven by wanting a clean-living space or doing what the alpha of the pack says; they are more interested in playing and having fun or cuddling. This means you don't have to worry as much about them doing something to test you as much as them doing something because you haven't been consistent, which is why it is so important to know how you are going to reward your Cavachon.

During the day, you can reward a successful trip outside by playing for a few minutes. At night, a successful trip could result in a small treat (you don't want the puppy hyper anyway, so probably best to avoid night-time play). Over time, you will be able to go outside less often, and the puppy will understand that these trips outside are the times to use the bathroom. At some point, your puppy will even understand that they should tell you when they need to go outside (if there is too large of a gap between outings). Yes, this is a long way away, but it is the ultimate goal.

You want to build a positive relationship with your Cavachon, so punishing your puppy for accidents is discouraged. Cavachons are smart, but they won't understand the correlation between the waste and the punishment. In the end, the puppy's takeaway is that it should use the bathroom where you can't find it inside.

The Cavachon wants you to be happy – you are more fun when you are. They want to enjoy their time with you, so positive reinforcement is the best way to give your puppy attention.

Regular Schedule, Doggie Door or Newspaper

Determining the best way to get your puppy to go outside can be a challenge and a lot of it depends on your schedule. If you cannot be home to take your puppy out about once an hour, you will probably have to start with puppy pads.

Photo Courtesy of Olivia Hartnett

The recommendation

It is best to train your puppy outside, even if there is some indoor training in the beginning. Making the kind of time required to do this in the early days can seem like a full-time job, but that is part of the price you pay for having a puppy you get to train and bond with from the beginning. Ultimately, the goal is to have the puppy only use the restroom outside, so you want to minimize how long a puppy is allowed to use the bathroom inside your home. The longer you wait, the harder it will be for the Cavachon to understand why the rules have changed.

How to transition to the outdoors

If you have to start with some indoor training (particularly in winter), you can start moving the training outside a little bit at a time. Place a small puppy pad in the area where you want the puppy to start going in your yard, but also work to train your puppy that it is alright to go on other things outside too. After a while, you can get rid of the puppy pad inside, teaching the puppy that it is no longer allowed to go in your home.

Leash training is also a great way to transition. Having the leash on indicates to the puppy that it is time to do some business. Then you can either go for a walk or out to the backyard. The puppy will know that this is a sign to go, then enjoy the rest of the time outside.

It's All On You – Cavachon Just Want to Please

Cavachons are people pleasers – they really just want to see you happy, and they are content. Well, if you are happy and spending time with them, they are content. They may not be quite as easy to train as some dogs, but they do not have to be the nightmare that people often associate with housetraining a small dog because the Cavachon wants you to be happy. As long as you are consistent and positive, your puppy will figure it out and start doing things your way.

If your Cavachon continues to go inside, you need to examine how you and the family have been training the puppy. It is likely that there is an inconsistent approach or mixed signals. That doesn't mean pointing fingers, but it does mean making sure everyone understands that they need to work the same way.

CHAPTER 9
Socialization and Experience

Even though Cavachons are naturally personable and friendly, they need to be socialized early in their lives to keep them from suffering from Small Dog Syndrome. They need to learn how to interact with dogs and people. By making time to have your puppy interact with others, the experience will help bring out the affable traits of your Cavachon. If you start when the puppy is young, your dog will realize that other dogs are fun and enjoyable and that strangers can be almost as enjoyable as family.

Benefits of Socialization

Socialization is a critical part of training because Cavachons can develop Small Dog Syndrome if they don't learn that other animals and people are fun. As the name suggests, small dogs can develop behavioral problems when they are not properly trained or socialized. For example, a small dog is typically allowed to do more than a large dog would be allowed to do. If a small dog jumps up on someone, they are less likely to be reprimanded for it than a large dog. It can lead to your dog growing up to try to bully other dogs, such as barking relentlessly at other dogs or acting aggressively. It can also mean your dog goes too far in the other direction if you are overprotective. They learn that the world is a dangerous place and that they should be terrified of everything.

The Cavachon can be a fantastic dog, but they need a bit of guidance when it comes to dealing with other creatures (even humans) because they can learn to be afraid if socialization is neglected. They can also get to be very skittish if they are left in a home most of the time without any type of interaction. Even though they can be homebodies, escaping the mundane is something they will appreciate. It will also make them tired, so you won't need to do as much work yourself. Getting out and doing new activities teaches your puppy that the world is a safe place, making them more relaxed when you take them out in public.

It's easy

Cavachons are people pleasers, so it should not be too difficult to teach them that other dogs can be fun. For a small dog, they will learn remarkably fast that other dogs and people are great too. They are predisposed to loving being with others. You can use this to help them get accustomed during play dates and walks.

You do want to keep the initial visits with other dogs in safe environments because they are rather little. Starting with dogs that are calm and mellow will help to build your puppy's confidence. When they get a bit older, you can expose them to other more excitable dogs, but in the early days, you want to make sure they feel comfortable and safe with play time.

People should be very easy, but you will need to make sure they understand the rules of playing with the puppy too. This is particularly true for the rules that the puppy should not be picked up or fed people food. Most of the interaction with people should be on the puppy's level. This should not be particularly hard as most people are not prone to picking up someone else's dog, but it is always good to make sure everyone plays by the rules so that the puppy knows what to expect.

Problem arising from lack of socialization – small dog syndrome

The primary concern with any small dog breed from lack of socialization is the development of Small Dog Syndrome. This problem isn't life-threatening, but it will reduce the quality of life for your Cavachon if the puppy isn't properly socialized when young. Not all small dogs develop it, but it isn't a problem that you will have with a big dog.

Photo Courtesy of Sarah Bewick

Small Dog Syndrome develops because people often treat a small dog differently than a larger breed. You are much more likely to be over-protective of them and to try to keep them from harm than a larger breed. Something about their size makes you feel compelled to want to keep them safe, whereas with a larger breed you know that the dog will be alright. In addition to being overprotective, you are much more likely to let a little dog get away with more because it is "cute" when a little dog does something. For example, a little dog jumping on someone is not going to cause any harm, but you would crack down pretty hard on a large dog that does the same thing. This disparity in treatment is very bad for your little dog.

By consistently applying the rules to your little dog and exposing the puppy to the same kinds of expectations that you would with a larger breed, you are really training yourself as much as the puppy. The Cavachon learns that they are safe, and you will learn that little dogs can be treated just like a big dog. Don't try to constantly protect your puppy from everything because that trains your puppy to be either scared or aggressive. Instead, let the puppy explore as much as you would allow a larger breed. Obviously, if you are out for a walk and encounter a dog that seems aggressive, be as protective with the little dog as you would with a big one – and that means not picking up the dog. Simply keep your puppy away from the aggressive dog. Then the next friendly dog you encounter, let your puppy sniff noses so that the puppy realizes that most dogs are alright.

Photo Courtesy of
Vicki Cowan

Why genetics matter

Genetics play a huge role in your puppy's developing personality. With a designer breed, there are a lot more variables because the breed is not established, and each litter is going to be different. The best way to gain an understanding of your puppy's likely personality is to find out as much as you can about both of the parents. The personalities of the Cavachon puppy's parents are probably going to be reflected in the puppy. Of course, the puppy will probably favor the personality of one or the other, but you will at least get an idea of how sociable and trainable your new family member will be in those early days. Having an idea of the parents' personalities will help you plan for training your puppy. If the parents are a little shyer or active, you can plan accordingly.

Overcoming shyness

Though not entirely common, it is possible that your little Cavachon may be a bit shy in the beginning. The puppy should be the one to initiate interaction with you. The whole family will need to make sure to sit back at a comfortable distance, letting the puppy come up to you when they are ready.

You will want to be calm and gentle when interacting with a shy puppy. Make sure the children understand that they need to be calmer and quieter around the puppy. If they are feeling boisterous, have them play in an area away from the puppy until they are calm enough to interact with your shy Cavachon. If your children cannot sit still or do not want to wait for the puppy to approach them, it will be best to keep them away from the puppy until your Cavachon is comfortable interacting with you and any other adults in the home.

Socialization with calm, friendly dogs in a familiar environment will help your puppy realize that other dogs are not so scary. With everything being so much bigger than the puppy, it is easy to understand how they might be intimidated. Mature adult dogs can be a positive calming influence.

Common Problems

Cavachons that take after the King Charles Spaniel parent could be more active and excitable than those that take after the Bichon Frise parent. You will need to train your puppy not to bark so much. The barking usually occurs when your dog is out for a walk, so watch for this when you first begin leash training. If you don't want your adult Cavachon to bark at everyone and everything that passes by, you will want to start training your puppy to be quieter on a walk. Socialization can help tone down the barking as well.

Properly Greeting New People

Your little puppy is going to look like a stuffed animal, and that means that there will be people who want to pick up your Cavachon. These are not the people who should be around in the puppy's early days, or if they are, they need to be told not to pick up the dog. The puppy should always be allowed to approach strangers at their own pace. Interacting with people should be a fun experience, and that means making sure your Cavachon feels comfortable and safe.

Photo Courtesy of Jenna Lovatt

Photo Courtesy of Vicki Minamyer

Behavior Around Other Dogs

As the kind of dog that just wants to play and have fun, as long as you start to socialize your puppy early, they should be very agreeable around other dogs. If you neglect socialization, are overprotective during interactions, or let your puppy get away with things, this could result in your puppy developing Small Dog Syndrome.

Instead, make sure to have your puppy meet dogs that you already know well. The dogs should already have proven that they like other dogs too. Keeping the interactions in a controlled and friendly environment will help your puppy feel safe around other dogs. They will naturally want to play and have fun, so you just need to encourage that affability to have a fantastic, friendly Cavachon.

CHAPTER 10
Being A Puppy Parent

"New owners tend to be so happy they have a cute little puppy, they forget to set boundaries. This leads to the puppy developing bad habits early on. Most people don't realize that the more they strive to have an obedient puppy, the more the puppy will love and respect them."

Linda Kaiser

www.smoochmypups.com

Having a puppy around the home can be a lot of fun. From their energy to the completely different take on their surroundings, puppies can make us rethink how we see the world. This is coupled with a lot of work, though. They still have everything to learn, and that means messes and mild destruction as your Cavachon learns. It is a time that is both incredibly cute and entirely frustrating.

Photo Courtesy of Paul O'Flynn

*Photo Courtesy of
Juli Voelker*

It is unbelievably easy to bond with Cavachon because they crave the attention and time of people. They will pick up on your emotions and react accordingly. If something makes you nervous, your Cavachon will probably sense that pretty early on and will react to that. They are going to follow you everywhere, and they are going to be sad while you are gone. It won't take long until your days revolve around your puppy, and it will be difficult to imagine living without the little fuzzball.

Staying Consistently Firm

Those absolutely adorable eyes are going to try to persuade you to go easy on them. It is your job to stay strong, firm, and say "No." Your puppy has to learn that you are serious. There cannot be exceptions because your Cavachon is going to be able to quickly figure out what caused you to give in. All it will take is trying it again later, and pretty soon you will be wrapped around your puppy's little paw.

To train any dog, you have to be consistent. To train a smart dog, you have to be incredibly firm as well. They are able to figure out cause and effect, and they will use that against you every chance they get. Once you make one exception to the rules, your Cavachon is going to try to make that exception the new norm.

Yes, it is difficult and tiring. That is why you have to plan ahead and know how to react. Cavachons react very well to positive reinforcement that doesn't require food, which means keeping a cool head and giving lots of praise for good behavior, no matter how small. In the end, you will have a fantastic, loving, and happy companion who knows how to behave.

Possible Problems with Cavachon

Photo Courtesy of Linda Cate

The biggest problem with Cavachons is the potential development of Small Dog Syndrome. They are so cute and fragile-looking that you are likely to treat them significantly different than you would treat a larger breed. You really need to let your puppy learn and figure things out the way you would allow a larger puppy to learn. Do not make them think that the world is a scary place, and definitely don't let them get away with things that you would not allow a larger dog to do. You do not want them thinking that they are the boss or that they can intimidate other dogs. This isn't a good quality in any dog, and it is generally something that starts in the puppy's early days.

You may find that your puppy wants to chase smaller animals and bark more when you are out walking. Just because your puppy isn't going to be able to pull you along does not mean that you should allow the aggressive behavior to go unchecked. You don't want your Cavachon chasing something out into the street if the puppy escapes the leash, nor do you want them thinking they can intimidate other animals.

Playtime!

This is going to be the part of the day that you really look forward to because it is going to be a lot of fun with a Cavachon. They want to play with you and just enjoy whatever it is you are doing. After a short training session, you are going to be free just to chill or play, whatever you are in the mood to do. Your Cavachon is going to be onboard for pretty much anything. Playing with a Cavachon puppy is also unbelievably adorable because they look like fuzz balls with eyes bouncing around after toys or chasing you as you crawl around.

Photo Courtesy of Debbie Conquest

Your puppy is going to be less fond of being alone. If you have to leave your puppy alone for a few hours, make sure to take the time to play for a bit as soon as you can. Regular playtime should be part of your schedule, but especially after time away, you should make sure to dedicate some attention to your puppy.

Training can be part of play – after all, they are just happy to be with you. Do remember that puppies cannot train for long, sustained periods. They are going to need short sessions in the early days. Focus on the basics, and over time, you will be able to lengthen training sessions and add some of the more entertaining tricks.

CHAPTER 11
Living with other dogs

"Cavachons love company and live well in a pack. I personally own three different breeds, the Cavachon being one of them, and they all adore each other."

Jenna Lovatt

www.pawfectcavachons.co.uk

Cavachons tend to be very gregarious and affable dogs that love people and other canines alike. They act like the little stuffed animals that their appearance suggests, so they aren't known for being territorial or aggressive. Since they hate to be alone, having another dog at home is advisable for those times when you have to go out.

Getting your new Cavachon familiar with your other dogs will be important, and the approach will vary based on if you have a puppy or an older Cavachon. Typically, you aren't going to have to worry about much, but you will still want to give the dogs time to get to know each other before you start leaving them alone together. Since your Cavachon is likely to do whatever the other dog wants, it will not pose much of a threat to any dog established as the alpha.

Introducing Your New Puppy

Any new dog should be introduced on neutral ground, including a puppy. This can help remove or minimize any territorial feelings your current canine has at home. Neutral ground lets your dog feel more at ease as you bring in a little bundle of fuzzy energy into the more laid-back life your dog has lived to that point.

As your dog begins to feel more comfortable around the puppy, you can start to prepare to head home. Arriving at your home as a pack will help make the new addition feel less threatening to the established order in your home.

Though there will be an established sense of familiarity, it does not mean there is an inseparable bond. Your puppy should be secluded

Photo Courtesy of
Kate Harvey

from the other dogs unless you or another adult is around. If you have children, make sure they understand that they cannot have the puppy around the other dogs without an adult present to supervise. Having a puppy space will help your new Cavachon feel more relaxed when she gets tired. This area should be set up and established well ahead of your puppy's arrival.

None of your other pets' toys or items should be in the puppy's area. Having toys and items of another dog can be particularly problematic as it can create unnecessary tension between your dog and the new puppy. Cavachons are not known for being destructive, but all puppies chew on things and you do not want your puppy chewing on the items of your other pets, especially dogs. That could be viewed as a challenge by your dog and could inspire unhealthy interactions with the puppy. When your Cavachon puppy is out of the designated puppy area, you need to keep a constant eye on the puppy so that your dog's things are not chewed on by the puppy. Your puppy should not be able to interact with anything that belongs to the other dogs in your home. Toys and other items should be stored while the puppy is out of the designated space; make sure to keep the food bowl out of the puppy's reach too.

When it is time to feed the dog and puppy, always feed them in different locations. Food is one of the greatest causes of disharmony between dogs, and it is tension that you can easily avoid by always keeping your dog and puppy eating in areas away from each other. As time passes and your puppy becomes more mature, you may be able to start feeding them near each other, but that should not happen in the early days. Make sure you plan for this before your puppy arrives. If you have the puppy's space away from where you feed your current dog, that will minimize tensions between the two.

One of the most important things you need to do when you bring a puppy home is to make sure you have time scheduled every day to play and interact with your dog or dogs without the puppy. They are going to feel a little nervous about the new addition, so one-on-one time with them will let them know that you still love them and that the puppy is not their replacement. Be prepared for some jealousy when you arrive home and your dog realizes that the puppy is there to stay. Keep your previous schedule with your dog in place as much as possible. For example, your puppy training time should not happen when you are usually out for a walk with your dog. Any established rules for your dog will need to apply to your puppy too. If your dog isn't allowed on the couch, neither is the puppy. Be consistent in the application of all rules so that you don't make your older dog feel resentful or unhappy about the new addition to the family.

As long as you are consistent with how you treat your dog and your puppy, there can be a world of benefits from already having a dog in the home. Your dog can help with training your puppy, let the puppy know what the rules are, show the puppy where to use the bathroom, and generally be an assistant in training. Depending on your dog, working dogs are also likely to help keep the puppy in line in a firm but gentle way. Your dog probably isn't going to be as caught up in how adorable the puppy is either, making it a great line of defense in making sure the puppy is socialized and learns how to behave. It is fine for your dog to scold your puppy, but make sure that there is no harm being done. Essentially, your dog can be a puppy babysitter after they are comfortable together.

If your dog is not interested in helping, that is also fine, particularly for senior dogs. They just want to relax and enjoy themselves, and adding a puppy to their day is already going to be trying enough. It is fine if they don't particularly care for the puppy, as long as there is no animosity or snappy behavior from your dog. Don't force the roles on your dog and puppy. Let them establish a relationship that they can both agree on, and the home will be a much more peaceful place.

Playful Dog Mentality

Given their adorable appearance and desire to play, it is all too easy to give in and let something slide with your Cavachon. It will be much more fun to play than to train, but you can't give in, especially with another dog in the house. All of the existing rules must be applied equally to all dogs to keep peace in your home. If your dog can't do something, neither can the puppy. Just because your Cavachon gives you the puppy-eye look, pleading you to offer food from your plate, don't do it. Your Cavachon will be able to tell that you are weak to their charms, and this is going to be very upsetting if you do not treat your other dog the same way.

Photo Courtesy of Vicky Minamyer

There is also the potential problem of your Cavachon and dog getting a little too rowdy as your puppy gets older. The more stamina your puppy develops, the more likely your dogs are to want to run around the house. Make sure that they have ample time to play outside so that this is not a problem. Over time, you can play with both your older dog and your mature puppy at the same time, helping them to play a little calmer when it is just the two of them.

Biting, Fighting, and Puppy Anger Management

Cavachons are known for being fun-loving companion dogs, but all puppies bite as they learn the rules. It is something you are going to need to plan to train your puppy not to do. Like all other training with your Cavachon, you should be calm and level-headed, despite the pain those pointy, little teeth can cause. They don't know better. Firm, consistent training and positive encouragement will go a very long way to teaching your puppy not to bite.

A bigger risk is the development of Small Dog Syndrome. They are so small and adorable, it is easy to feel that you need to be protective of them. This is true when it comes to aggressive animals, but for the most part, you need to let your puppy socialize normally with other dogs and people. Don't pick up your Cavachon and carry the puppy around because that is both bad for your Cavachon's health (your puppy really needs exercise) and teaches the puppy that it is in charge. Train and socialize your Cavachon like you would any larger breed. Exercise some caution, but don't be overprotective. Definitely don't let your puppy get away with anything. Your dog will be more than happy to help, otherwise, you may find yourself facing more than just some less than desirable behavior from your other dog too.

Raising Multiple Puppies at Once

Having more than one puppy at a time is a unique challenge that can easily result in feeling like you are spending all of your time training. Raising one puppy is a full-time job; raising more than one is a full-time job with constant over time. If you choose to raise two Cavachon at once, it will not be as challenging as many other intelligent dogs because it will be easier to apply the rules to both and have them listen (as long as you are consistent and provide positive reinforcement).

Consistency is going to be absolutely essential. You cannot allow exceptions to the rules because, with two smart puppies, exceptions doubly undermine your authority and training. It is going to be difficult in those first weeks and months because you are going to want to play more than to train. The puppies will agree. Once the rules have been established and the puppies know you are serious, it will actually be pretty easy. You will still need to be consistent, but your puppies aren't likely to try to outsmart you or push the boundaries. They just need to know that the boundaries are there and are not moving.

You are not going to have much of a personal life for a while after bringing more than one puppy into your home. Taking care of your puppies is going to be all you have time to do in those early days. This approach is necessary to teach your puppies to behave and to socialize.

You will need to spend time training them both together and separately. This means more training sessions. Since they are individual dogs, they need time with you one on one. This will help you understand their unique personalities, little quirks, and other things about your puppies that you won't notice if they are constantly together. You also need to establish bonds with your puppies as individuals, which you can't do if they are constantly together. Having someone play with the other puppy will minimize jealousy too. Cavachons aren't prone to being alone and will likely want to play with each other, you, and anyone else around instead of being split up, but you will need to give them individual time.

Even Cavachon puppies are likely to fight at one point or another. It may just be harmless wrestling, but you will need to keep an eye on it to make sure that it is just playful. They may be establishing who is dominant, although Cavachons don't tend to worry about this as much as many other breeds. As long as it doesn't become a serious fight, let them work things out.

When training, you are going to need to minimize how much they distract each other when you train them at the same time. To do this, you are going to need to remove all of your own distractions. If you are taking care of their food, stay focused on the task until the puppies are eating. If you are preparing for a walk, don't do anything else until the walk is complete – once the leashes are out, get the puppies out the door as soon as possible. Your Cavachons are watching and learning. If they are excited about walking and suddenly have to wait while you text someone back or walk away to use the bathroom, you now have two very excited puppies with no outlet. They don't understand patience, so they are likely to let that energy out on anything nearby. They may take to pouncing on you or other pets in their excitement, which could be a tripping hazard if nothing else.

The way your puppies act is pretty much a reflection of how you have trained them. If you are consistent and firm, you will find that training gets easier. If you allow yourself to be constantly distracted, your puppies are going to realize this and take advantage of your lost focus.

Photo Courtesy of Diana Smith

CHAPTER 12.
Training Your Cavachon Puppy

Cavachons are a relatively smart breed. While they don't have the intellect of a German Shepherd or Border Collie, they are much smarter than most small dogs. Given that they come from breeds that are used mostly for companionship, it is somewhat surprising how smart the Cavachon can be. This can be both a fantastic thing and a reason to be cautious with your puppy. Smart dogs may learn quickly, but that means they can also learn things that you don't want them to learn.

Remember those little eyes are observing you and learning from what you do.

A Gentle Consistent Approach

Being consistent and gentle with your Cavachon puppy is the best way to succeed in the training. Because they want to have fun and enjoy their time with you, they are going to notice the kinds of behaviors that they do that create a positive reaction from you. They will notice this, but they will also notice how you aren't doing the same thing every time.

Staying consistent and firm is going to be a real challenge because these puppies are absolutely adorable. At the end of a long day, you are going to be inclined to just let them get away with small things. But you can't. No matter how tired you are, the rules have to always apply. Similarly, no matter how cute your puppy is being, the rules must still apply. Even if you just want to cuddle, you have to take a few minutes to train at the regular time. Schedules and rules are incredibly important in those early days.

Training is the mechanism to teach your puppy everything it needs to know about being a part of your family. Once your puppy has had time to learn and adjust, you can become more flexible – but that will be down the road.

For now, be prepared to be a constant teacher and trainer. This is how your puppy will learn about the expectations and pack. For as laid back as they are, even Cavachons like to know the pack hierarchy. This is part of their socialization and is something you will need to do to keep your puppy from developing Small Dog Syndrome.

Photo Courtesy of
Alison Murphy

Gain Their Respect Early

All dogs operate on the respect they have for the people in their lives. If they don't respect you, even a delightful little dog like the Cavachon will take advantage of the situation. That is simply canine nature. Without respect, your dog is not likely to listen to you. That does not mean that you should make your puppy fear you. It just means that you need to be firm and consistent.

Respect is earned, not forced, especially with such an agreeable breed as the Cavachon. Your puppy is going to want to make you happy. If you are firm and consistent in your training and enforcement of the rules, your puppy will get comfortable pretty easily. The hierarchy will be obvious, and that is usually enough for a Cavachon puppy.

The best way to develop a strong bond is through positive interactions. This means using positive reinforcement to get your puppy to act a certain way. Treats are alright, but telling your puppy what a good boy he is will be more than enough for a Cavachon to want to repeat an action. The time you spend in training is a time where your puppy learns to listen to you and bond. Your Cavachon is really just looking to spend time with you. Once the rules are established, this will be much easier.

Operant Conditioning Basics

Operant conditioning is simply the scientific term for actions and consequences. This is exactly what your Cavachon needs to learn – how certain actions gain positive consequences.

Since this is a friendly, affable breed, positive reinforcement works wonders. Smarter dogs know that a happy human is more enjoyable to be around, and Cavachon will also crave the praise that comes with the correct actions. Hearing that they have done well goes a lot further to encourage the behavior you want than using negative reinforcement.

There are two types of reinforcements for operant conditioning;
- Primary reinforcements
- Secondary reinforcements

You will use both during Cavachon training.

Photo Courtesy of Jade Moore

Primary Reinforcements

A primary reinforcement gives your dog something that it needs to survive, with food being one of the most common. However, positive social interaction is another primary reinforcement type and is the one you should opt to use more often. Cavachons love to be with you, so hearing praise is highly effective during training.

Initially, you may want to rely on primary reinforcements because your Cavachon will not need training to enjoy them. Food is generally something that is wonderful to have outside of meal time, and extra time and attention from you is always welcome. However, do be careful about striking a balance with food. Mealtime and playtime should never be denied to your Cavachon, no matter how poorly the pup performed during training. These are essentials to living, so you have to provide them – that is not negotiable. It is the extra treats and playtime that are up for negotiation and what you use to reinforce good behavior.

Always err on providing too much attention and affection, while being relatively stingy on the treats. Your Cavachon is not going to get very big, and you do not want the puppy to learn to overeat.

Secondary Reinforcements

Photo Courtesy of Victor Hood

When you take up a new hobby or physical activity, you do a lot of repetition to improve. The improvement that comes with repetition is secondary reinforcement. Pavlov's experiment with dogs is probably the most widely-known example. Pavlov tested dogs, teaching them to associate the ringing of a bell with meal time. They were conditioned to associate the bell with a primary reinforcement – food. The same thing is true with cats and can openers; they may come to associate the sound with food and come running toward the kitchen when they hear it.

Secondary reinforcements work very well with Cavachons because your puppy will associate the trigger with something that is required. This reinforces that particular behavior. Dogs who are taught to sit using a treat only will automatically react by sitting when you offer a treat, even if you don't tell them to. They know that the treat in your hand means that they should sit. Of course, this is not the type of training you want to reinforce because you want your Cavachon to sit on command, not when you have food in your hand. This is why it can be tricky to move to secondary reinforcers.

Fortunately, you have the advantage with Cavachons of using praise. They do enjoy food, but not nearly as much as your attention and positive interaction.

Toys can also be used to get your puppy to act the right way. If you have a regular schedule that you can adjust to give your Cavachon a little extra attention for doing really well, that is just as effective, if not more so, for this particular breed.

Sometimes punishment is required, but it really should be used sparingly. When your Cavachon does something you don't like or that it shouldn't do, ignoring your puppy is far harsher than any other kind of punishment because the puppy craves interaction. All you need to do is put the puppy back in the designated puppy area and walk away, but not out of sight. No matter how much your puppy whimpers, just ignore the behavior, no matter how much you want to give in. This reinforces that you are not happy.

To reinforce behavior, the reward or punishment must be almost immediate. With too much time between the misbehavior and the punishment, your puppy is not going to understand why the punishment has happened and could associate the incorrect action with the punishment.

If the puppy whines and whimpers to let you know that it is time to go outside and you fail to act, that is not the puppy's fault, so you should not be punishing your Cavachon. You have to learn the puppy's signals as much as the puppy needs to learn your instructions.

When praising or punishing your Cavachon, keep eye contact the entire time. This may require holding the scruff of your puppy's neck gently to force it to look into your eyes (obviously only for punishment, as your puppy will look you in the eyes and wag that little tail when receiving praise).

Why Food Is a Bad Reinforcement Tool

Cavachons are small, so overfeeding them is a serious concern. Since they are such a gregarious breed, it is best to use positive language and attention as the primary motivator during training. Treats can be used when you don't have much time or when it is the middle of the night and you are still house training the puppy. Other than that, it is best to stick to using praise and play.

Treats are alright in the early days because your puppy is growing and will likely expend a good bit of energy. This will give you time to train your puppy to enjoy the positive words as much as the treats. It will be easier for a puppy to understand to follow a treat for things like come or roll over, too. You can lead them with the treat and then hand over the treat when they succeed.

There are three basic commands where you will probably need treats – sit, stay, and leave it. Your Cavachon definitely will not understand the words in the beginning, so the treats are an easy way of showing that your puppy has done the right thing. "Leave it" will be the most difficult to do without treats, so even if you teach this one a little later, using treats is still alright.

Photo Courtesy of Alison Murphy

Small Steps to Success

Those first few weeks and months are going to seem long because your puppy is not going to understand much in the beginning. This is particularly true with the house training. You will need to start slowly and build up a daily routine. Being in a new home, with new people and sounds, is going to be somewhat scary and exciting. Either way, it is definitely going to be a huge distraction for your newest addition. Once your puppy is more familiar with the place (and therefore a bit bored by it), it will be easier to get the point across.

Still, you should start training as soon as your puppy arrives – small steps. You want to plant the seed, then have your puppy come to understand exactly what you want from the regular visits outside. As your puppy gets familiar with the place, you can also start crate training. The crate should be a safe place that is familiar and just the puppy. Over time, you will probably cease to need the crate as your Cavachon is going to want to sleep in the same room as you or another member of the family, but at least in the early days when the puppy will be alone, the crate should be a safe place to rest at the end of the day.

Why Trainers Aren't Always Necessary

Cavachons don't tend to need trainers. They bond very well with their families and don't tend to want to be alpha. As long as you can dedicate a considerable amount of time to basic training, then you really won't need a trainer for a Cavachon. They are more interested in spending time with you than someone who doesn't live with them. That doesn't mean they won't love the extra socialization – it just isn't really necessary.

If you have the patience and positive outlook required to be firm and consistent, you should be able to manage the basics without much help. Since Cavachons also don't tend to be a destructive breed, just a bit clingy when you are around, you don't need to keep them mentally occupied all of the time like other intelligent dogs. They are smart, but not intelligent enough to require constant attention and activity. Their lower energy level means that just hanging out with you is enough to keep them happy.

CHAPTER 13
Basic Commands

Cavachons are smart, so if you want your puppy to learn lots of tricks, that is definitely an option. They will prefer things that are close to you, like high five and rollover, but you should be able to teach them fetch and other tricks that mean leaving your side.

Before you get to those though, you need to start with the basics.

Why Size and Personality Make Them Ideal Companions

Training is absolutely necessary for Cavachon. They can be alright without much training, but you want to make sure that your Cavachon listens to you. Basic training will make them responsive to tasks you want them to do, sometimes for their own safety. Actions like sit and stay are useful, but leave it can be a lifesaver for your Cavachon. Given their size, it won't take much cleaning supplies or hazardous foods to be a serious health hazard to your dog. If you see your Cavachon eating something that it shouldn't, you want to be able to tell the dog to "leave it" and drop the food.

If a Cavachon is well-trained, the people around you will enjoy the canine that much more. Watching this little living stuffed animal do tricks is its own type of entertainment, and all of the attention will make your puppy very happy. Since they tend to love everyone, training will pay off within months. If you don't train your Cavachon, do make sure to socialize your dog. Training is always recommended for dogs, but your Cavachon will probably still be a good companion if you don't want to do more than the basics.

Picking the Right Reward

The right reward for Cavachon is praise, but in the early days, you will likely need to use food. Of course, keep food to a minimum and switch to praise and additional playtime as soon as possible. Extra petting can also be a great reward.

Photo Courtesy of
Ffion Roberts

As you gain respect (which shouldn't take too long), you can start to use that in the training too. Respect won't be part of the basic training because it will take some time to build, but by the time you reach the last command ("leave it"), you may have a little leverage from your Cavachon's respect for you. Respect can be a great motivator. At the end of every training session, give your puppy extra attention, some extra belly rubs, or additional play to show how pleased you are with your puppy's progress.

Successful Training

Training focuses on learning commands. By learning only to respond to the reward and not the command, the training is not considered to be successful.

Respect is generally the key to successful training. The work you and your puppy do together will help develop respect (remember, respect comes from consistent, firm training). It will take a while for your Cavachon to learn to feel respect for you, even though your puppy will be quite fond of you very quickly. At this point, your puppy does not have the necessary understanding or relationship to have respect quite yet. Once it is established, you will be able to switch the reward system to something fun instead of food.

Though you can't rely on it yet, petting and attention should be part of the training. Over time, your puppy will be able to start correlating the desired behavior with the additional attention. Once your puppy begins to understand, training will get easier. Associating the extra attention and petting as a reward encourages your puppy to look at playtime as a great reward. No matter how much they enjoy food, more time and attention from you is something that your Cavachon will probably love even more.

Basic Commands

Puppies need to learn five basic commands. By the time your puppy understands how to react to the commands, the Cavachon will understand the purpose of training. That will make it easier to train your puppy to do more complicated tricks.

Follow the list in the order provided. Sit is considered the most basic command, and it is something that your Cavachon already does naturally. That makes it easier for the puppy to understand what you want. Leave it is the most difficult command, so you will need to build up your puppy's understanding during training. Dropping something is not a natural reaction for your dog, especially if the puppy has food, so you are working against instinct with this one. It will take longer to train for this one, so have the necessary tools already in place to improve your chance of successfully training this command.

The following are basic guidelines for training.

- Everyone in the home should be part of the training because your Cavachon needs to learn to listen to everyone.
- Have a designated training area and make sure there are no distractions for you or the puppy. Leave your phone and other mobile devices out of sight so that your attention is given completely to the puppy and training.
- Stay positive and excited about the training. Your Cavachon puppy is going to pick up on your emotions, so if you are enthusiastic, your puppy will be too.
- Be consistent as you teach.
- Bring a special treat to the first few training sessions, like cheese or a small piece of meat.

Once you are ready, start working and bonding with your adorable little Cavachon.

Photo Courtesy of
Paul O'Flynn

Sit

After settling in with the special treat, start training. Sit will be relatively easy. Wait until your puppy starts to sit down, and say "Sit" before the motion is done. If your puppy finishes sitting, give praise and a little bit of treat. Naturally, this will make your puppy excited and wiggly, so you may need to wait for the excitement to settle before you try again. When your puppy calms down and starts to sit, repeat the process.

This will take several sessions, probably over the course of a couple of weeks, for the puppy to really understand the concept. Cavachons are smart, but following commands is an entirely new idea. However, once your puppy understands the purpose and how to react to the command, the puppy's brain will be working to connect your next command with the appropriate action.

Wait until your puppy can consistently follow your instructions before moving on to the next command.

Photo Courtesy of Elaine Myers

Down

Follow the same process for down. When the puppy starts to lie down, say "Down." If the Cavachon finishes the action, offer the reward. This will probably take less time once you start. Once your puppy demonstrates a mastery over the command, you can move on to the next command.

Stay

This one will be more difficult since your Cavachon is going to want to follow you everywhere. Be prepared for this one to take at least twice as long as sit because this is entirely counterintuitive to your puppy's nature and desire. It is also important that your puppy has mastered the other commands first.

Choose if you want your puppy to be sitting or down when you tell the puppy to stay. You will need to start with the puppy in this position for the rest of the training sessions until your Cavachon has mastered the command.

Tell your puppy to stay from either a sitting or lying position. When you do, place your hand in front of the puppy's face. Wait until the puppy stops trying to lick your hand before you begin again.

When the puppy settles, take a single step away. If your puppy does not move, say stay and offer a treat along with some praise.

The reward indicates that the command is over, but you need to signal that it is also complete by repeating the command. The puppy must learn to stay until you indicate that it is okay to leave. Once you give the okay, do not offer any more treats. "Come" should not be used as your okay word as it is another basic command.

Repeat these steps, creating more distance away from the puppy as the puppy shows the ability to stay.

Once your puppy understands this command, start training your puppy to stay even if you are not moving. Extend the amount of time required for the puppy to remain in one place so that the puppy understands that stay ends with the okay command.

When you feel confident that your puppy has the command down, you can move to the next.

Come

Your puppy needs to have mastered the previous three commands before starting this one. The other two commands do not require the puppy to have experience with commands to start (it is easier to train the puppy already has an understanding of what commands are and how the puppy should react).

Before you start with come, decide if you want to use "Come" or "Come here." You and the family must be consistent in using just one of those two commands. Once you know which one to use, make sure the rest of the family knows too.

- Leash your Cavachon.
- Tell the puppy to stay and move away.
- Say your chosen version of the come command and give the leash a gentle tug. As long as you did not use the term to indicate that the stay command is over, your puppy will start to understand the new command. If you used the term to indicate the end of stay, this will just confuse your puppy as your puppy will associate "Come" with a part of "Stay" and not its own command.

Repeat these steps, building a larger distance between you and the puppy. When the puppy understands the command, remove the leash, and start close again. If the puppy seems to have problems without the leash, you can provide visual clues, such as patting your lap. Your Cavachon will definitely want to sit in your lap. Provide the reward as soon as your puppy reaches you.

Leave it

This is going to be one of the most difficult commands you will teach your puppy because it goes against both the Cavachon's instincts and interests. Your puppy wants to keep whatever he or she has, so you are going to have to offer something better. It is essential to teach it early though, as your Cavachon is going to be more destructive in the early days. You want to get the trigger in place to convince the puppy to drop things.

You may need to start teaching this outside of the training arena as it has a different starting point.

Start when you have time to dedicate to the lesson. You have to wait until the puppy has something in his or her mouth to drop. Toys are usually best. Offer the puppy a special treat. As the Cavachon drops the toy, say "Leave it," and hand over the treat.

This is going to be one of those rare times when you must use a treat because your puppy needs something convincing to drop the toy. For now, your puppy needs that incentive, something more tempting than what he or she has to learn the command.

This will be one of the two commands that will take the longest to teach ("Quiet" being the other). Be prepared to be patient with your pup.

Once your puppy gets it, start to teach leave it with food. This is incredibly important to do because it could save your Cavachon's life. They are likely to lunge at things that look like food when you are out for a walk, and being so low to the ground, they are probably going to see a lot of food-like things long before you do. This command gets them to drop whatever they are munching on before swallowing it.

Where to Go From Here

Cavachons may not be the fastest learners, but they learn very quickly for a small dog – and you may be pleasantly surprised at just how quickly they pick up on these basic commands. If you find that you are eager to train your Cavachon more to make your cute little fuzzball a real entertainer, there are plenty of tricks that are perfect for these delightful little dogs.

Make sure that your Cavachon knows these commands before you move on to some of the more complex tasks. Some will build on these basic tricks, while others are unrelated. However, training with these tricks will give you the foundation you need to advance to something more. If you find that your Cavachon has trouble doing these, it might be best to get these down and then just play with your Cavachon. If you still want to train your dog, make sure to train in sessions that your dog can manage without pushing too hard.

As your Cavachon ages, you can teach tricks that really highlight what you both enjoy. If you want to ham it up, there are plenty of tricks that will make people melt to watch your dog do them. Others you can enjoy with just your dog so that it doesn't try to take up the entire bed or eat food that falls on the floor. There are plenty of practical tricks that your Cavachon can learn once the basics are learned.

CHAPTER 14
Nutrition

Just as you need to pay attention to what you eat, you need to be careful about what your Cavachon eats. This plays a significant role in your dog's health and energy levels. Fortunately, you have a lot of control over what your Cavachon eats, just make sure that you don't leave anything down on their level – and don't give in to those cute eyes.

From the day your Cavachon comes home, you need to make sure they get a balanced diet. This ensures that you and your Cavachon can continue to enjoy having fun together well into your dog's later years.

Why a Healthy Diet Is Important

Photo Courtesy of Megan Roe

Cavachons do not have a particularly high energy level – they love lounging on the couch just as much as a walk or romp outside. Because they are not inclined to being hyper or bouncy, you cannot let them have too many calories. They will not be able to work off lots of extra treats, and certainly not highly processed human food. A healthy, well-balanced diet is absolutely necessary to ensure your Cavachon doesn't put on weight that will lower the dog's life expectancy.

Be aware of your Cavachon's eating habits. Make sure that the food your Cavachon gets is a balanced diet that is matched with regular exercise. It is good to be aware of how many calories your canine consumes daily and to ensure that your dog gets the right vitamins and nutrients.

Commercial Food

Commercially-sold dog food is incredibly flawed. Since the food is entirely processed, your dog will not be able to process all of the nutrients, even if the dog food contains them. Unfortunately, most people do not have the time to make dog food as often as they would need to, even for a dog as small as the Cavachon. At least that is the impression most people have; it seems like just one more chore to the day.

If you really do not have time to do a little additional cooking for your Cavachon, take the time to read the bags and purchase one of the premium-grade commercial dog foods. This will help make sure that your dog gets the right nutrients. You can add a few extra ingredients to the commercial food to supplement any nutrients that you think may be missing. Not only can this supplement the nutrients, but your Cavachon will likely enjoy the extra taste, especially if it is juice, egg, or other foods you are eating too.

Preparing Your Food Naturally at Home

While it may take a bit more time every day, you can plan on it only being an extra five or ten minutes a day to cook your Cavachon's meals. If you are careful about what you eat, you can even add a little extra of your own meal to your dog's food. Of course, since your Cavachon's dietary needs are different than yours, you can mix regular dog food with some human food to ensure your Cavachon is getting all the proper nutrients it needs. Keep in mind the foods that could be deadly to your canine, and make sure you don't give these to your dog if you are making it for yourself.

While you shouldn't feed your Cavachon before you eat (you don't want your dog to get accustomed to being the first one fed because it can give the impression it is the alpha of the pack), you can feed your Cavachon at the same time as when you eat. The best home-cooked meals need to be planned so that you know your canine has the necessary nutrients. Canines usually need about 50% of their diet to be from animal protein, such as poultry, oily fish, and organ meats. Roughly a quarter of their food should have complex carbohydrates, and the remaining quarter should be fruits and vegetables (being aware of the foods your Cavachon shouldn't be fed). Pumpkins, apples (without seeds), green beans, and bananas are great foods for any canine, and they have a smell that will be very appealing too. The real benefits of these foods is that they can make your dog feel full faster.

Puppy Food vs. People Food

Photo Courtesy of Olivia Hartnett

Cavachon puppies should always have food that is specific for puppies. Do not feed your Cavachon puppy people food believing it will be fine because it will be both a bad precedent and unhealthy for your puppy. It will quickly become an expectation; your Cavachon will expect to eat the same food you do, and you are likely to find your puppy refusing to eat the dog food.

It is best to make your dog's food if possible, but you have to be careful to make sure that your puppy gets the necessary nutrients. Their bodies have special needs as they grow, and the first few months are particularly critical. If you can make the food while keeping in mind all of the nutrients needed, it will be best for the puppy for the first year, then you can switch to dog food. This could also be better for your wallet as well.

Dieting, Exercise, and Obesity

Dogs aren't dieters; they should have a regular diet that they stick to. It is your responsibility to create a regular eating schedule and stick to it. If you create an expectation for treats and snacks, that is going to be a part of your Cavachon's regular diet, and even a lovable pup like the Cavachon is going to expect and demand it. There are many reasons why it is a terrible habit to develop, and one reason you should switch to other types of positive reinforcement as early as possible. Instead of treats and snacks, let your Cavachon curl up with you while you watch something or spend some extra time playing. The extra exercise will be much healthier and just as welcome as any food you can offer.

A healthy diet and regular exercise are essential for your Cavachon, and it is better for you too. It will help give you a reason to get out of the house and exercise while also helping your dog stay at a healthier weight. Having a regular exercise and playtime routine to reward your canine is also cheaper, making it a much better system for both of you.

Warning About Overfeeding and the Right Caloric Requirement

Given how cute they are and their small stature, you have to be extra careful to watch your Cavachon's caloric intake, especially during the transition to adulthood. Cavachons aren't as notorious for being food crazy as other dogs, but they can learn to be if you rely on food to reward them. Overfeeding your dog is not a reward, but a hazard. Keep your dog's health in mind while feeding and training to ensure that you aren't overindulging the pup.

Regularly checking your Cavachon's weight can help ensure you aren't overfeeding the pup. You should be able to use your own scale to monitor their weight. Step on the scale by yourself and check your weight, then step on the scale with your Cavachon. Then you just need to subtract your weight from your weight with your dog. Make sure to be honest about your own weight though because you don't want to overestimate your dog's weight. Counting calories can be very time-consuming (which can help you keep from giving your dog so many treats). Still, you should be aware of roughly how many calories your Cavachon consumes in a day.

Photo Courtesy of
Sue Tabner

CHAPTER 15
Grooming – Productive Bonding

Cavachons are easy to groom, even the ones that are not hypo-allergenic. While Bichon Frises are hypoallergenic, it is not guaranteed that your Cavachon will be. Even if not, you still aren't going to need to spend hours grooming your pup every week. Caring for your Cavachon's coat is incredibly easy, and your canine will love the extra attention. Their fur can get a little matted if not properly tended to though, so do make sure that you make it a regular part of your weekly routine, or at the very least a bi-weekly activity. Given their size, it won't take you very long to brush them and move on to something more enjoyable. Regular brushing will also keep the amount of dog hair you have around your home and on your furniture to a minimum.

Beyond taking care of your Cavachon's coat, you will need to take care of a few other grooming aspects. Their teeth will need to be cleaned regularly, as well as their ears. When giving your Cavachon a bath, make sure you do not get shampoo or water in your canine's ears (this is true for all dogs, but worth mentioning a few times to make sure you are careful while cleaning your Cavachon). Fortunately, cleaning your Cavachon isn't too difficult as they are likely to do what you want them to do. Even if they do decide to struggle, they are pretty easily subdued so that you can clean them safely.

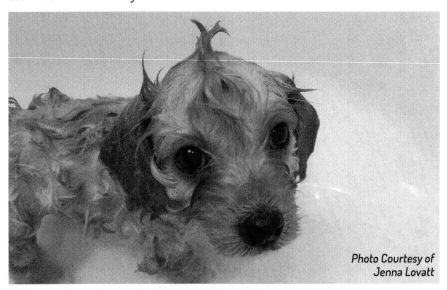

Photo Courtesy of
Jenna Lovatt

Managing Your Cavachon's Coat – It's Easy

Brushing your Cavachon is actually a pretty relaxing activity, and one that you may find helps relieve some stress for you and the pup. Most Cavachons will eat up the attention that you are giving them, particularly if you talk to them while you are brushing. It probably isn't going to take long until your Cavachon starts to look forward to brushing (unlike bathing), so making it a part of a regular weekly schedule will likely make your dog very happy. With their small stature, it isn't going to take you particularly long to brush them either.

Photo Courtesy of Debbie Conquest

Puppy

You may find that brushing a Cavachon puppy is a bit of a challenge, as your puppy is probably going to be incredibly wiggly and excited. They will take the brushing as a sign that it is time to play, and there is a good chance they will nip and try to knock the brush out of your hands. Of course, it is going to require your patience and gentle coaxing to get them to stop. Although it will be cute at first, you still want to get them to stop that behavior so that you can complete the task – it will be much less cute when they are older and still think that brushing is playtime instead of cleaning time.

Making brushing a weekly endeavor will be more time-consuming in these early days because of your puppy's desire to play instead. As your puppy learns better, it will be a lot easier to complete the activity. To help, brush your puppy after a tiring walk when the Cavachon does not have enough energy to try to play.

Adulthood

Brushing an adult Cavachon should be a weekly endeavor. As long as you stay on top of it, an adult Cavachon is only going to require a few minutes of brushing. You may want to brush your Cavachon a couple of times a week in the spring and summer if you notice that your dog is prone to shedding. Cavachons that take after the Cavie side are much more likely to shed, so you will want to keep the fuzz down through regular brushing.

Your Cavachon may need to get a haircut from time to time as they do have medium length hair.

Bathing: Watch the Ears, Shampoos

Bathing is going to be a fairly regular activity, but not anything that will be a significant burden. Brush your Cavachon before the bath.

While cleaning your Cavachon, take the time to inspect your dog's ears to make sure there aren't any infections. Given that they are a mixed breed, you want to make sure they remain healthy, especially since ear infections are a problem for some Cavachons. Check to make sure that the insides of their ears are dry, something that should be fairly simple. If you do get water in your dog's ears, monitor them for a few days to make sure that they don't get infected.

Trimming the Nails

This is something that may be best left to a professional, as a young Cavachon may not sit still enough for you to manage the task. Take some time to learn from the professional - what the person does to keep your Cavachon relaxed and calm. You can start trying to keep your Cavachon calm in a similar manner, and at some point when you are successful, you can try cutting the dog's nails yourself. You will need to be very careful that you do not cut too much. If your Cavachon has black toenails, you will need to be extra careful.

Puppies should have their nails cut weekly, and adults will need it monthly. If you walk your dog on concrete, this could have a wearing effect, so you may not need to trim them nearly so often. Do keep an eye on the length of your Cavachon's nails and cut them when they get too long, even if you do walk on harder surfaces that wear the nails down.

Brushing Their Teeth

This one is a monthly task to ensure that your dog's teeth stay healthy from puppyhood all the way through their golden years. The task isn't likely to be as much of a headache for a Cavachon as it is for many dogs. There is also the added benefit of making your dog's breath fresher. If you notice plaque buildup, you may need to brush your canine's teeth more often.

Cleaning Ears and Eyes

Cavachons tend to get ear infections, so you do need to make sure to keep an eye on them. Not all Cavachons have this problem since they are a mixed breed, but you want to be careful just in case. Check your Cavachon's ears for waxy buildup or infection when you bathe your dog, or even during a regular brushing. It only takes a few seconds and can really help keep your dog healthy.

To take care of your Cavachon's eyes, regularly check them (like when you are brushing your dog) to make sure there isn't any dirt or fur in the eyes. If there is dirt, use an eyewash approved by your vet to clean the eyes. Carefully clean or cut any dirty fur. They do shed tears, which is normal. However, you will need to carefully clean the fur stains that result from the regular tears

*Photo Courtesy of
Ffion Roberts*

CHAPTER 16
Basic Health Care

Cavachons are fantastic companions, and since they aren't pure breeds, they are less prone to health issues. As long as you take good care of your dog, you are likely to have a fantastic little companion for a long time. Most of these are things you should already know to do, so take this as a good reminder. Other tasks are specific to your Cavachon, and you should make sure to add the tasks to your schedule.

Over the course of your Cavachon's life, you will need to make sure to do some basic preventative care so that your little dog does not suffer from easily preventable problems. Most of these problems are universal to canines, not just Cavachons, so you can apply many of these measures for your other dogs. Come back to this chapter periodically to make sure that you remember to take proper care of your canine.

Fleas and Ticks

Cavachons have sensitive skin, so flea bites can cause minor infections. You should use regular flea and tick treatments to reduce problems with these parasites. During regular brushings, check your Cavachon for bites. You may need to treat the bites if you find them.

If you take your Cavachon into the woods, you will need to check over your canine once you return home, just like you should check yourself. This is also true if you go into a field or area with tall grass where ticks are likely to live. You will need to comb through the Cavachon's fur, taking a close look for this parasite to make sure your dog does not have them either attached to their skin or moving up the fur. You should brush your Cavachon a second time within 24 hours in case you missed a tick. With their thicker, longer fur, it will be harder to find these nasty parasites, so you will want to double check. If you find a tick has attached itself to your Cavachon, treat the bite.

During regular brushings, keep an eye out for fleas. It will be more difficult to find them; it is more likely that you will see the bites instead of the fleas. That is why it is important to pay attention when you brush your Cavachon. If you notice your dog scratching often, take the time to check to make sure fleas are not the problem. Even if you don't go to places that are likely to have fleas, the Cavachon's low stature makes

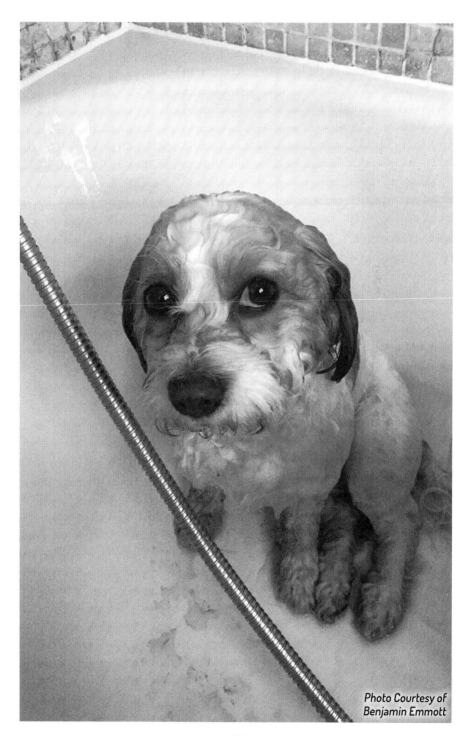

Photo Courtesy of
Benjamin Emmott

it an easy target for fleas even in nicely groomed yards. If you regularly treat your dog and still find there is a problem with fleas, you may need to change the product you use.

If you would like to use a natural flea and tick preventative, you should spend a few hours researching your options. You can also increase the number of baths you give your dog, but this should only be a temporary solution when your Cavachon is actually having a problem with one of the two insects. With their sensitive skin, you don't want to dry it out through frequent bathing. Make sure to verify the product's efficacy before you make any purchases for natural remedies.

Flea and tick treatment should be a monthly occurrence. If you need to, set a reminder on your phone to make sure you complete the treatment every month.

Worms and Parasites

While these are much less of a problem, you still want to protect your little companion from them. There are many parasitic worms that could be a problem:

- Heartworms
- Hookworms
- Roundworms
- Tapeworms
- Whipworms

The following are possible symptoms that your Cavachon is suffering from one of these worms. If you notice any of these symptoms, schedule a visit with the vet to have your canine checked out.

- If your Cavachon seems unusually lethargic
- Patches of fur begin to fall out (this will be noticeable if you brush your Cavachon regularly), or if you notice patchy spots in your dog's coat
- If your Cavachon's stomach becomes distended (expands), set up an appointment immediately to have him or her checked. Your Cavachon's stomach will look like a potbelly.
- Your dog begins coughing, vomiting, has diarrhea, or has a loss of appetite

Many of the signs of worms can be symptoms for other problems, at least in the early stages. A visit to the vet could find that one of these par-

*Photo Courtesy of
Dorren Bowen*

asites is the problem, or it may be something else. Whatever the issue, it is best to get your dog checked out as early as possible.

If your Cavachon has hookworms or roundworms, you will need to visit your own doctor as well. Skin-to-skin contact with your Cavachon can pass the parasite on to you, so if your Cavachon has a problem, you and others in your home might have the same problem. Everyone will need to be treated to make sure that you don't perpetuate the ailment.

Heartworms are a serious problem for your Cavachon, and they are something you should be actively preventing in your dog. Heartworms can be deadly. There are medicines that can help your dog if the vet diagnoses heartworms as an issue. There are also preventative medicines to keep your dog from suffering the problem in the first place.

Benefits of Veterinarians

You should have an annual visit to the vet to take care of required shots and for your Cavachon to get a regular checkup. Just as you should be visiting yearly, so should your dog.

Since Cavachons are not a particularly high energy dog, the vet visits will help detect any potential problems you may not notice. Of course, with as often as you interact with your Cavachon, any changes in behavior could be an indication that something is wrong, in which case you should take your dog to the vet outside of the annual visit. This should not alter the regular visits, though.

Health checkups are also good for ensuring that your dog is aging well. Given that they are not a pure breed, it can be more difficult to identify problems since it is harder to know what your dog is at greatest risk of having (unless you keep tabs on the parents and know what kinds of problems they have as they age). The vet can also help you figure out ways to help you work around common canine issues, such as arthritis. They can make suggestions about things you can do to manage prob-

Photo Courtesy of Lorraine Hamilton

lem so that you don't end up having less time with your dog. Things like shorter walks and more indoor playtime (instead of walks or long hikes) can help keep your dog healthy and active as your Cavachon ages. In the end, it is worth changing the routine to keep your Cavachon happy and healthy well into their golden years.

Holistic Alternatives

Wanting to use a more holistic approach to caring for your Cavachon is understandable, but it requires considerable research before you commit to it. You do not want to take any unnecessary risks with your little companion. Unverified holistic medicines are not only a waste of time, they are a potential health risk.

Before starting use of a holistic medicine or treatment, consult your vet. You can also discuss options with your vet that are more established than an untested or unverified holistic alternative. Read what scientists have had to say about each alternative. There is a chance that some of the more established treatments are better for your Cavachon than something holistic.

Vaccinating Your Cavachon

The vaccination schedule for your Cavachon is the same as it is for most dogs.

The first shots are required between 6 and 8 weeks following the Cavachon's birth. You should find out from the breeder if these have been taken care of and get the records of the shots:

- Coronavirus
- Distemper
- Hepatitis
- Leptospirosis
- Parainfluenza
- Parvo

➢ These same shots are required again at between 10 and 12 weeks of age.

➢ These same shots are required again between 14 and 15 weeks old, as well as his or her first rabies shot.

➢ Your dog will need to get these shots annually after that. Your Cavachon will also need annual rabies shots.

Ensuring that your dog gets her regular shots can help keep your newest family member happy and healthy for many years.

CHAPTER 17
Health Concerns

Given the short history of the Cavachon and the fact that it is not a pure breed, trying to guess as to what ailments a dog is likely to inherit is tricky at best. Looking over the few decades that they have been around, there are a few ailments that have shown up more than others. However, the best way to keep your Cavachon healthy is to look for the ailments that are common to both of the original breeds. Fortunately, both of the parent breeds are well established, making it easier to monitor for certain common ailments in the two breeds. Both parent breeds also tend to be relatively healthy, which means your dog is likely to be with you for a very long time.

A Wild Card

Since Cavachons are not a pure breed, they do not have the same established health concerns as pure breeds. Since the dog can take on the genetics from either side, you should know what kinds of health problems are common for both Cavies and Bichon Frises.

All designer breeds are essentially wild cards when it comes to hereditary ailments they may have. You have to monitor them for a much wider range of potential problems, but they are also less likely to have those problems. The only real difference between a designer breed and a mutt is that designer breeds are bred for particular traits. Like mutts, designer breeds that come from healthy parents are less likely to have the problems that are common to the original breeds.

Where you can go wrong

Before getting into hereditary ailments, there are two non-hereditary aspects that should be considered – diet and exercise. If you take good care of your Cavachon, being mindful of what your dog eats and how often your dog exercises, the chance of some hereditary ailments is reduced. Your dog will also have a better quality of life, regardless of their genetics.

Diet

The easiest thing you can do to keep your Cavachon healthy is to make sure that your canine's diet is appropriate for the dog's size

*Photo Courtesy of
Glynis Smith*

and activity level. Since they are small and only have a medium level of energy, your Cavachon is not going to need a lot of food. Not giving your dog treats and letting him eat off of your plate is going to be harder on you, so keep in mind that you are potentially reducing your dog's lifespan by giving in.

With one of the parent breeds having some gastrointestinal problems, there are plenty of reasons for you to be more careful about what you feed your Cavachon. If nothing else, you do not want to be cuddling up with a dog that constantly farts and vomits. You can avoid this by keeping your dog on a healthy diet.

Exercise

Cavachons just want to be with you, which can make it easy to be sedentary but that isn't healthy. Given their medium energy level, it is pretty easy to ensure they meet the proper activity level. A couple of nice walks and playing around the house is all they really need. A solid 30 minutes of activity per day is generally enough to keep them healthy if you are careful about their diet.

Both parents are prone to a particular heart disease (mitral valve disease). This does increase the risk of your Cavachon having it. Making sure your dog gets exercise every day can go a long way in reducing the risk of heart diseases. Regular exercise is easy to do and an easy way to keep your canine healthy for the majority of her life.

Importance of breeder to ensure a healthy cavachon

Being aware of the health of the parents and the diseases that are known to be a problem for them will help you know what to monitor for in your Cavachon. There are diagnostic tests conducted on both parent breeds. While there are no required tests for Cavachons, if the parents have a history of certain problems, you can have the tests conducted on your Cavachon. It is always best to be safe than sorry.

If possible, find out what the health and history of your Cavachon's parents. This is the only way to be able to prepare for what likely ailments your Cavachon may inherit. Knowing what to watch for as your dog ages can help you get the right help early enough to extend your dog's life.

Common Diseases and Conditions

Since the history of the Cavachon is too short for a reliable set of common risks, you should watch for the health problems that are common for both of the parent breeds.

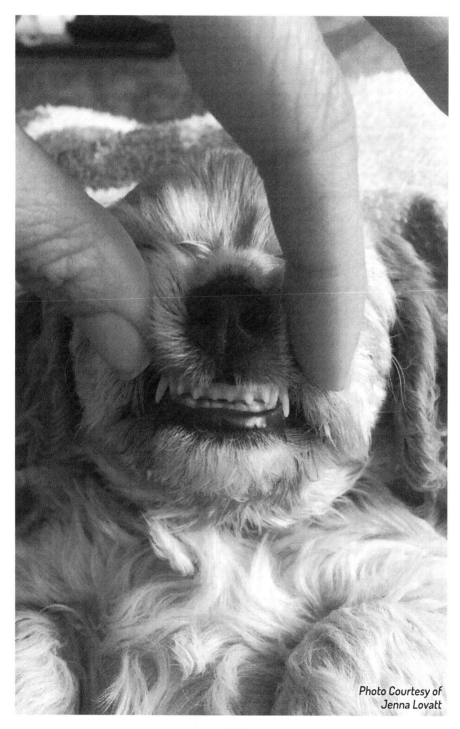

*Photo Courtesy of
Jenna Lovatt*

Cavalier King Charles Spaniel

Cavies have a few common ailments, and you should find out if your Cavachon's Cavie parent had any of these issues:

- Canine hip dysplasia (major health problem)
- Entropion (minor health problem)
- Mitral valve disease (major health problem)
- Patellar luxation (minor health problem)
- Retinal dysplasia
- Syringomyelia (major health problem)

All of these diseases are common in the breed, but they have significantly different levels of health concerns and not all of them are life-threatening.

Bichon Frise

Bichon Frises also have a few common ailments you should ask the breeder about:

- Bladder infections and stones (common problem)
- Cancer (less frequent problem)
- Dental disease (common problem)
- Eye diseases, particularly cataracts (common problem)
- Gastrointestinal problems (less frequent problem)
- Liver shunt (less frequent problem)
- Metabolic diseases (less frequent problem)
- Patellar luxation (common problem)
- Mitral valve disease (less frequent problem)
- Skin and allergy issues (common problem)

Bichon Frises have five common problems that are usually easy to manage through proper grooming, diet, and activity. They do not tend to be life-threatening. The other five problems are much more serious, but less common than the other five. You will want to keep an eye on your Cavachon to make sure your dog is not showing symptoms of the five less frequent but more serious problems.

Prevention & Monitoring

With genetic issues being more difficult to predict, you want to take as many preventative measures as possible. Having a regular exercise routine and a healthy diet can help minimize many ailments, both hereditary and environment based. Act in your Cavachon's best interests. They will follow your lead, so if you are too sedentary, they will be too. If you constantly offer treats, they will eat them.

Monitoring your Cavachon for signs of ailments common in the parents can help keep your dog's health from deteriorating as quickly as it might if left untreated. Yes, you will have a wider range of ailments to watch for, but it is worth it. Even if your Cavachon is less likely to suffer from common problems, it isn't guaranteed that your dog won't inherit some issues. Paying attention to your dog and setting up regular vet visits can do a lot to make sure your dog is around for many years to come.

Photo Courtesy of
Lorraine Hamilton

CHAPTER 18
Your Aging Cavachon

Given how new this designer breed is, determining the average lifespan has not been well-established, and the potential range for their expected life expectancy is between 10 and 15 years. The more mindful you are about your Cavachon's exercise levels and diet, the longer your dog is likely to live. With such a large range for their life expectancy, it is important to know how healthy both parents are. By the time your Cavachon is 9, he or she is considered to be a senior dog, and you will need to start adjusting your dog's diet and exercise levels to accommodate the aging process as different systems slow down. Your sweet little pup is not going to be able to do all of the exciting things that you used to do together, but more time relaxing on the couch and just lounging on a nice spring day will be just as enjoyable.

Each Cavachon is an individual, and with the lack of established history, you are really going to need to adjust your schedule to accommodate your specific canine. The aging process may begin very slowly, almost imperceptibly. However, your Cavachon is going to try to keep doing everything you want to do because limitations are something to ignore. That is why it is so important to pay attention to your Cavachon at the 8- and 9-year mark. You don't want the little pup pushing beyond the limits of aging. It is incredibly easy to accommodate your aging Cavachon, and these years can be just as enjoyable (if a bit lazier) than the earlier years of your dog's life.

Senior Dog Care

Aging Cavachons are incredibly easy to care for because they will require far less exercise and playing. There will be a lot more napping and cuddling, which isn't too bad. If you want to sit and watch something, your Cavachon is perfectly happy with going out for a quick bathroom break and nestling down instead of taking a longer evening walk. Just make sure to have a little extra play time in your home because your Cavachon should not completely forgo exercise.

Exercise and diet are as critical during the senior years as they were when your Cavachon was a puppy. You can't now decide that your Cavachon has earned all of those treats you have been denying him or her all of the years simply because the canine is in the golden years.

Photo Courtesy of
Juli Voelker

Their little bodies are not accustomed to the treats you are tempted to give your dog, and your Cavachon certainly isn't able to exercise adequately to burn off high caloric treats. These cute, little, furry pups are not able to handle extra weight during this time.

If you notice that your Cavachon is having a difficult time on longer walks, you can reduce the length of walks and take more, shorter walks every day. Spend more time romping around the yard or home instead – your Cavachon will love that because it will be incredibly easy to flop down and sleep afterward, no waiting for the leash to be removed.

There are items that an older Cavachon will need regular access to, which could mean making some changes around the home.

- Set water bowls in a few places so that your Cavachon has easy access to water.
- Cover hard floor surfaces (such as tile, vinyl, and hardwood). Rugs and carpets that won't slip out from under your Cavachon are important to make sure your pup doesn't get hurt just by walking around the home.
- Add cushions and softer bedding for your Cavachon. This will make surfaces more comfortable while helping your little guy to stay warm. Remember, they do not handle cold very well, and the older they get, the easier it is for them to get cold. There are bed warmers if your Cavachon shows signs of achy joints or muscles.
- Increase how often you brush your Cavachon to improve circulation. This will help keep them a little warmer, as well as being a great way to spend time together when your Cavachon isn't capable of the more exciting excursions.
- Stay inside during extreme heat and cold. Your Cavachon may be healthy, but they aren't exactly a hearty breed when it comes to extreme temperatures.
- Use stairs or ramps instead of constantly picking your Cavachon off the ground. Constantly picking them up may be more convenient, but it is not healthy for either you or the dog. It is best to grant your Cavachon as much self-sufficiency as possible during their golden years.
- Avoid remodeling and rearranging your furniture. A familiar home is far more comforting and less stressful for an aging dog.
- If your home has stairs, consider setting up an area on a single floor for your dog and refrain from leaving that floor as much as possible. Your Cavachon is going to want to be wherever you are, and that includes going up and down stairs even if your dog isn't able to do it safely or without pain.

- Create a space where your Cavachon can relax and be alone if desired. Of course, it isn't very likely that your Cavachon is going to want much alone time, but in case your Cavachon becomes a bit of a curmudgeon, a little alone space will be quite welcome when he or she isn't feeling particularly well.

- Be prepared to let your Cavachon out to use the restroom more often. They will not be able to hold their bladders for as long.

- Diabetes is a concern since Bichon Frise are known to develop the disease if they do not have a healthy diet. It is certainly avoidable, but it does mean making sure your Cavachon continues to eat healthily.

- Arthritis is a concern for dogs just as much as humans. If your dog shows signs of the ailment, such as stiffness or pain after normal activities, it could be arthritis. You should take your pup to the vet to check and find out the best ways to help reduce pain. Do not give your dog the same medication you take because their systems cannot handle a full-strength pain reliever. Follow your vet's instructions and keep medication to a minimum since these dogs are very small and their bodies cannot handle large amounts of medicine.

- Gum disease is a concern on the Bichon Frise side. Be vigilant about brushing your Cavachon's teeth. Also, include gum checks during regular vet visits to make sure your Cavachon's mouth is healthy too.

Photo Courtesy of Megan Roe

- Loss of eyesight is common in all dog breeds (as well as in humans). Unlike humans, however, there really isn't a safe glasses option for dogs. Have your dog's vision checked annually. If your Cavachon is showing signs of deteriorating eyesight, make more frequent checkups so that you can adjust to help your dog navigate the home and walks better.

- Kidney disease is common in older dogs and is one that you really need to watch for in your aging Cavachon. If your pup is drinking more often and having regular accidents, this could be a sign of something more serious. Get your dog to the vet as early as possible if you notice this problem.

Nutrition

Since your little companion is not going to be able to exercise as much, it is necessary to change what they eat and how much. If you opt to feed your dog commercial food, make sure to find a healthy food for senior dogs. Find ways to reduce calories without sacrificing taste too. You don't want to give your Cavachon really bland food if that is not what your dog used to eat.

If you make your Cavachon's meals, reduce the fat in the food. More meat is good because your dog will need protein, but make sure it is healthier meat instead of fatty meats.

Exercise

This is going to be a lot trickier because it probably isn't going to be as obvious if your Cavachon is hurting. They are more focused on being with you and having fun than in how they are feeling, and this can cause them serious problems if they overexert themselves. Shorter walks at a higher frequency are a great way to keep your little guy active without pushing him past his limits. Increasing your time playing inside is just as effective because it will be easier to relax once playtime is over. You also won't be tempted to pick up your Cavachon to carry them home if you are already there.

Your Cavachon will probably start to gain weight in the later years, so you do need to be careful to make sure exercise levels match their caloric intake. Reducing activity is inevitable, but you should not stop entirely.

Fortunately, this is a pretty easy transition for Cavachons. They care more about being with their people than about getting out and about.

When you go out for walks, your Cavachon will probably spend more time sniffing and walking along at a slower pace. Let your dog do this because it is moving at a more comfortable pace. As tempted as you may be to pick your dog up, don't. Take the time to enjoy your surroundings instead of getting annoyed at the slow pace and frequent stops. It is a new type of curiosity for your dog, and he or she is finally stopping to smell the roses (or blades of grass and leaves). This is fine and can be just as enjoyable as those boisterous walks with a puppy.

Mental Stimulation

Cavachons are smart, so you should keep their minds active. You may not need to worry about them being destructive, but playtime and reinforcing training are still important. There is no such thing as too old for a Cavachon to learn new tricks either. Since they won't be able to take those long strolls anymore, this could be the perfect way to help them exercise while keeping their mind working. Games like hide and seek will be just as welcome, as your Cavachon will enjoy looking for you.

Regular Vet Exams

Just like you expect to go to the doctor more often as you age, your Cavachon will need to go to the vet more often. It isn't necessarily because of problems, but wellness checks should be more frequent just to make sure your dog is alright. Your vet can let you know if your Cavachon is either too active or not active enough given the dog's weight and current physical abilities. If your canine has sustained an injury and has kept it from you, your vet will be much more likely to notice the ailment.

Your vet can also make recommendations about activities and your Cavachon's schedule. For example, if your Cavachon has begun to pant more, this could be a sign of pain caused by stiff joints or something else. Changing the walks or how you play can help ease the pain. Your vet is a fantastic resource for learning a more physically comfortable range of activities during the later years of your dog's life.

Potential Old-Age Ailments

Chapter 17 covered the likely ailments your Cavachon may have or develop, and many of these will not show up until the later years. But old age also comes with its own set of ailments that are pretty universal across the canine world, such as arthritis. Be more aware of your Cavachon's behaviors because these could indicate that your dog is not as healthy as you think. Some symptoms will just be aging, while others could be something more serious. Keep an eye on your Cavachon and set up appointments if you notice anything strange or a shift if your Cavachon's personality.

Regular grooming is also important because you can see potential issues. By having established regular brushings, teeth care, and washings, you will be able to spot things that could indicate a problem. Your Cavachon's breath may get worse, which could be a sign of gum disease. Skin infections may be worse, requiring a change in shampoos, your brush, or something else. The bond you formed all of those years ago through brushing is definitely going to be a help now to keep your aging friend healthier longer.

Enjoying the Final Years

Your Cavachon's later years can be incredibly enjoyable because they will be a real couch potato. After a long day, you won't have to feel bad that you aren't up for a long walk. Turn on the TV and gently play with your Cavachon on the couch. Do a short training session of all the old familiar tricks, then kick back with a book. It is an incredibly mellow time that can make life a lot easier while also freeing up your schedule a bit.

Steps and ramps

Given the Cavachon's small stature, you are going to want to ease any old-age ailments by picking up your Cavachon at stairs and steps. Fight that urge because it is not helping your dog. By carrying your dog, you are speeding up the deterioration of your dog's muscles, meaning the dog's body will be less capable. That doesn't mean you should expect your canine to go up and down long flights of stairs daily, but don't pamper your pup for small staircases and easy to maneuver steps.

Enjoy the advantages

Cavachons are one of those dogs that are just as much fun in their senior years as when they are pups – perhaps more, if you aren't into training from scratch. They tend to retain that fun-loving, carefree attitude that people love. They are one of the few breeds that exhibit less change in old age because they are always happy to just lounge with you. They are people pleasers just as much in their later years as the early ones. If you want to train, they are game. If you want to kick back, just lend them your lap. About the only real change is that the walks will have to be shorter, but if you go out more often, that may be welcomed as it forces you to take breaks more frequently.

It is even possible that they will start to initiate relaxing sessions. They may let you know they just want to get on the couch and chill if they aren't feeling up for real activity. Being able to pick up on your social cues, they may know just want you need and try to convince you to rest no matter how busy you are. After all, if your best friend needs to rest on the couch, how can you say no?

What to expect

Your Cavachon probably isn't going to suffer from a fear that you are less interested in spending time with them. They will continue to be the happy, friendly little dog you have always loved, which is why you have to be careful. Your Cavachon's limitations should dictate interactions and activities. If you are busy, make sure you schedule time with your Cavachon to do things within those limitations. Your happiness is of utmost importance to your Cavachon, so let the little canine know you feel the same way about her happiness. It is just as easy to make an older Cavachon happy as a young one, and it is easier on you since relaxing is more essential.

Photo Courtesy of Victor Hood

Made in the USA
San Bernardino, CA
27 July 2020